GIOCONDA

THE WORKS OF
Signor Gabriele D'Annunzio

Crown 8vo, cloth extra, 6s. each.

I

The Romances of the Rose

THE CHILD OF PLEASURE. (Il Piacere.)   [*Ready.*
THE VICTIM. (L'Innocente.)   [*Ready.*
THE TRIUMPH OF DEATH. (Il Trionfo della Morte.)   [*Ready.*

II

The Romances of the Lily

THE VIRGIN OF THE ROCKS. (Le Virgini delle Rocce.)   [*Ready.*
THE PRODIGY. (La Grazia.)
THE ANNUNCIATION. (L'Annunziazione.)

III

The Romances of the Pomegranate

FERVOUR. (Il Fuoco.)
THE DICTATOR. (Il Donatore.)
THE TRIUMPH OF LIFE. (Il Trionfo della Vita.)

Also uniform with this play,

The Dead City

Translated by Arthur Symons. Price 3s. 6d.

LONDON : WILLIAM HEINEMANN
21 BEDFORD STREET, W.C.

$GIOCONDA$

B^Y *GABRIELE D'ANNUNZIO*

Translated by
ARTHUR SYMONS

NEW YORK: R. H. RUSSELL
MDCCCCI

Facsimile of the title page of the original edition.

Cosa bella mortal passa, e non d'arte

Leonardo da Vinci

GIOCONDA

By *GABRIELE D'ANNUNZIO*

Translated by
ARTHUR SYMONS

New York · HOWARD FERTIG · 1989

Published in 1989 by Howard Fertig, Inc.
80 East 11th Street, New York, N.Y. 10003

Library of Congress Cataloging-in-Publication Data
D'Annunzio, Gabriele, 1863–1938.
    Gioconda.
    Translated from the Italian.
    Originally published : New York : R.H. Russell, 1901.
    I. Title.
PQ4803.Z3G59   1989   852'.8   87-38137
ISBN 0-86527-382-0

Printed in the United States of America

FOR

ELEONORA DUSE

OF THE BEAUTIFUL HANDS

DRAMATIS PERSONÆ

LUCIO SETTALA

LORENZO GADDI

COSIMO DALBO

SILVIA SETTALA

FRANCESCA DONI

GIOCONDA DIANTI

LITTLE BEATA

LA SIRENETTA

---

*At Florence, and on the coast of Pisa,
at the present time*

GIOCONDA

THE FIRST ACT

*A quiet, foursquare room, in which the arrangement of
everything indicates a search after a singular
harmony, revealing the secret of a profound corre-
spondence between the visible lines and the quality
of the inhabiting mind that has chosen and loved
them. All around seems to have been set in order
by the hands of one of the thoughtful Graces. The
aspect of the place evokes the image of a gentle and
secluded life.*

*Two large windows are open on the garden beneath ;
through one of them can be seen, rising against the
placid fields of the sky, the little hill of San
Miniato, and its bright Basilica, and the convent,
and the church of the Cronaca, "la Bella Villanella,"
the purest vessel   Franciscan simplicity.*

A

*There is a door opening into an inner room, another
leading out. It is the afternoon. Through both
windows enter the light, breath, and melody of
April.*

SCENE I.

SILVIA SETTALA *and the old man* LORENZO GADDI *are
seen on the threshold of the first door, side by side,
as they both come into the fresh spring atmosphere.*

SILVIA SETTALA.

Ah, blessed be life! Because I have always kept
one hope alight, to-day I can bless life.

LORENZO GADDI.

New life, dear Silvia, good brave soul, so good and
so strong! The storm is over. Lucio has come back
to you, full of gratitude and of tenderness, after all
the evil. It is as if he were born again. Just now
he had the eyes of a child.

SILVIA SETTALA.

All his goodness comes back to him when you are
with him. When he calls you Maestro his voice
becomes so affectionate that it must make your heart
beat, the father's heart that you have for him.

LORENZO GADDI.

Just now he had the same eyes that I saw in him when he came to me for the first time and I put the clay into his hands. His eyes were gentle and wondering ; but from that moment his thumb was full of energy, a revealing thing. I have kept his first sketch. I thought of giving it to you on the day of your betrothal. I will give it to you in token of your new happiness.

SILVIA SETTALA.

Thanks, Maestro.

LORENZO GADDI.

It is the head of a woman crowned with laurels. I remember there was rather a bad model there. As he worked, he hardly looked at her. Sometimes he seemed absorbed, sometimes anxious. There came out of his hands a sort of confused mask, through which one half saw I know not what heroic lineaments. For some moments he remained perplexed and discouraged, almost ashamed, at the sight of his work, not daring to turn to me. But suddenly, before letting it out of his hands, with a few touches he set a crown of laurel about the head. How it delighted me ! He wanted to crown in the clay his

own unaccomplished dream. The end of his day's
work was an act of pride and of faith. I loved him
from that instant, for that crown. I will give you
the sketch. Perhaps, if you look at it closely, you
will discover the ardent face of Sappho, that ideal
figure which, only a few years later, he was able to
bring to perfection, in a masterpiece.

SILVIA SETTALA.

[*Listening eagerly.*] Sit down, sit down, Maestro ;
stay a little longer, I beg of you. Sit here, by the
window. Stay a few minutes longer. I have a
thousand things to tell you, and I do not know how
to tell you one of them. If I could overcome this
continual tremor ! I want you to understand. . . .

LORENZO GADDI.

Is it joy that makes you tremble ?

[*He sits down near the window.* SILVIA, *leaning
back against the window-sill, remains with
her face turned towards him : her face is seen
against the blue air, the little hill standing out
in the background.*

SILVIA SETTALA

I do not know if it is joy. Sometimes everything
that has been, all the evil, all the sorrow, and even

the blood, and the wound, all melts away, vanishes, is wiped out into oblivion, is there no more. Sometimes everything that has been, all that horrible weight of memory, thickens and thickens, and grows compact and opaque and hard as a wall, like a rock that I shall never be able to surmount. Just now, when you spoke to me, when you offered me that unexpected gift, I thought: "Ah, now I shall take that gift in my hands, that morsel of clay into which he cast the first seed of his dreams, as into a fruitful soil; I shall take it in my hands, I shall go to him smiling, bearing intact the better part of his soul and of his life; and I shall not speak, and he will see in me the guardian of all his goods, and he will never go away from me any more, and we shall be young again, we shall be young again!" I thought that, and the thought and the act were mingled in one, with an incredible ease. Your words transfigured the world. Then, do you know, a breath passed, a vapour, the merest breathing, a mere nothing, and cast down everything, and destroyed everything, and the anxiety came back, and the dread, and the tremor. O April!

[*Suddenly she turns to the light, drawing a deep breath.*

How this air troubles one, and yet how pure it is!

6 GIOCONDA

All one's hope and despair pass in the wind with the dust of flowers. [*She leans out, calling.*] Beata! Beata!

LORENZO GADDI.

Is the little one in the garden?

SILVIA SETTALA.

There she is, she is running about between the rose-bushes. She is wild with delight. Beata! She has hidden herself behind a hedge, the rogue. She is laughing. Do you hear her laughing? Ah, when she laughs, I know the joy of flowers when they are filled to the brim with dew. That is how her fresh laughter fills my heart to overflowing.

LORENZO GADDI.

Perhaps Lucio too hears her, and is consoled.

SILVIA SETTALA.

[*Grave and trembling, leaning towards the Maestro, and taking his hands.*] You think then that he will really be healed of all his wounds? You think he will come back to me with all his soul? Did you feel that, when you saw him, when you talked with him? What did your heart say?

LORENZO GADDI.

It seemed to me, just now, that he had the look of
a man who begins to live over again with a new
sense of life. He who has seen the face of death
cannot but have seen in that instant the face of
truth also. The bandage is taken off his eyes. He
knows you now wholly.

SILVIA SETTALA.

Maestro, Maestro, if you deceive yourself, if it is a
vain hope, what will become of me? All my strength
is worn out.

LORENZO GADDI.

But what is there now to fear?

SILVIA SETTALA.

He wanted to die; but *the other*, the other woman
lives, and I know that she is implacable.

LORENZO GADDI.

And what could she do now?

SILVIA SETTALA.

She could do anything, if she were still loved.

LORENZO GADDI.

Still loved? Beyond death?

SILVIA SETTALA.

Beyond death. Ah, if you knew my anguish! It
was for her that he wanted to die, in a moment of
rage and of delirium. Think how he must have loved
her, if the thought of me, if the thought of Beata,
could not restrain him! Then, in that awful
moment, he was her prey wholly; he was at the
height of his fever, of his agony, and all the rest of
the world was blotted out. Think how he must have
loved her!

[*The woman's voice is subdued but lacerating.*
The old man bows his head.

Now, who can say what took place in him, after the
blow, when the mist of death passed before his soul?
Has he awakened without memory? Does he see an
abyss between his life as it renews itself and the part
of himself that he left behind in that mist? Or else,
or else the image has risen again out of the depths,
and remains there, against the shadow, dominant, in
indestructible relief? Tell me!

LORENZO GADDI.

[*Perplexed.*] Who can say?

SILVIA SETTALA.

[*In a sorrowful voice.*] Ah, now you yourself dare

not console me any longer. Then, it is so? There is no help?

LORENZO GADDI.

[*Taking her hands.*] No, no, Silvia. I meant: who can say what change is brought about in a nature like his by so mysterious a force? Everything in him speaks of some new good thing that has come to him. Look at him when he smiles. Just now, yonder, before you left him to come out with me, when he kissed those dear hands of yours, did you not feel that his whole heart melted into tenderness and humility?

SILVIA SETTALA.

[*Her face slightly flushed.*] Yes, it is true.

LORENZO GADDI.

[*Looking at her hands.*] Dear, dear hands, brave and beautiful, steadfast and beautiful! Your hands are extraordinarily beautiful, Silvia. If sorrow has too often set them together, it has sublimated them also, perfected them. They are perfect. Do you remember the woman of Verrocchio, the woman with the bunch of flowers, with the clustering hair? Ah, she is there!

[*He perceives, from the look and smile of* SILVIA, *that there is a copy of the bust on a little cupboard in a corner of the room.*

So you have realised the relationship. Those two hands seem of the same blood as yours, they are of the same essence. They live—do they not?—with so luminous a life that the rest of the figure is darkened by them.

SILVIA SETTALA.

[*Smiling.*] Oh, young, always young in soul!

LORENZO GADDI.

When Lucio comes back to his work, he ought to model your hands the first day. I have a fragment of ancient marble, found in the Oricellari Gardens. I will give it to him, that he may chisel them in that, and lay them up like a votive offering.

SILVIA SETTALA.

[*A cloud passing across her forehead.*] Do you think he will come back to his work soon? Will he wish to? Have you spoken of it with him?

LORENZO GADDI.

Yes, just now, when you were not there.

SILVIA SETTALA.

What did he say?

LORENZO GADDI

Vague, delicious things, a convalescent's dreams.
I know them. I too was once ill. It seems to him
now as if he has lost hold of his art, as if he had no
longer any power over it, as if he had become a
stranger to beauty. Then again it seems to him as if
his thumbs had assumed a magic force, and that at a
mere touch he can evoke forms out of the clay as
easily as in dreams. He is somewhat uneasy about
the disorder in which he fancies his studio was left,
on the Mugnone yonder. He asked me to go and
see. Have you the key?

SILVIA SETTALA.

[*Anxiously.*] There is the caretaker.

LORENZO GADDI.

How long is it since you were there?

SILVIA SETTALA.

Since *this* began. I never had the courage to go
back again. I feel as if I should see the stains of
blood, and find traces of *her* everywhere. She is
still mistress there. That place is still her domain.

LORENZO GADDI.

The domain of a statue.

SILVIA SETTALA.

No, no. Do you not know that she had a key?
She came and went there as if it belonged to her.
Ah, I have told you, I have told you; she lives, and
is implacable.

LORENZO GADDI.

Are you sure that she came back, after what
happened?

SILVIA SETTALA.

Sure. Her insolence has no bounds. She is without pity and without shame.

LORENZO GADDI.

And he, Lucio, does he know?

SILVIA SETTALA.

He does not know. But he will surely know it
sooner or later. She will find a way of letting him
know.

LORENZO GADDI.

But why?

SILVIA SETTALA.

Because she is implacable, because she will not
relinguish her prey.

[*A pause. The old man is silent. The woman's
voice becomes harsh and tremulous.*

And the statue, the Sphinx, have you seen it?

LORENZO GADDI.

[*After a moment's hesitation.*] Yes. I have seen it.

SILVIA SETTALA.

Was it he who showed it to you?

LORENZO GADDI.

Yes, one day last October. He had just finished it.   [*A pause.*

SILVIA SETTALA.

[*In a trembling voice, which almost fails her.*] It is wonderful, is it not? Tell me.

LORENZO GADDI.

Yes, it is exquisitely beautiful.

SILVIA SETTALA.

For eternity!

[*A pause, burdened with a thousand undefined and inevitable things.*

THE VOICE OF BEATA.

[*From the garden.*] Mamma! Mamma!

LORENZO GADDI.

The child is calling you.

SILVIA SETTALA.

[*Starting up, and leaning out of the window.*]
Beata! Ah, there she is; my sister Francesca is
coming across the garden; she is coming here with
Cosimo Dalbo. Do you know? Cosimo has returned
from Cairo; he arrived at Florence last night. Lucio
will be delighted to see him.

LORENZO GADDI.

[*Rising to go.*] Good-bye, then, dear Silvia: I shall
see you perhaps to-morrow.

SILVIA SETTALA.

Stay a little longer. My sister would like to see
you.

LORENZO GADDI.

I must go. I am late now.

SILVIA SETTALA.

When shall I have the gift you promised me?

LORENZO GADDI.

Perhaps to-morrow.

SILVIA SETTALA.

No perhaps, no perhaps. I shall expect you. You
must come here often, every day. Your presence

does us good. Do not forsake me. I trust in you,
Maestro. Remember that a menace is still hanging
over my head.

LORENZO GADDI.

Do not fear. Keep up your courage!

SILVIA SETTALA.

[*Moving towards the door.*] Here is Francesca.

SCENE II.

FRANCESCA DONI *enters, goes up to her sister, and
embraces her.* COSIMO DALBO, *who follows her,
shakes hands with* LORENZO GADDI, *who is on the
point of going out.*

FRANCESCA DONI.

Do you see whom I am bringing? We met outside the gate. How are you, Maestro? Are you
going just as I come in? [*She shakes hands with the
old man.*]

SILVIA SETTALA.

[*Holding out her hand cordially.*] Welcome back,
Dalbo. We were expecting you. Lucio is impatient
to see you.

COSIMO DALBO.

[*With affectionate solicitude.*]   How is he now ? Is
he up ?   Is he quite well ?

SILVIA SETTALA.

He is convalescent ; still a little weak ; but getting
stronger every day.   The wound is entirely closed.
You will see him in a minute.   The doctor is with
him ; I will go and tell him you are here.   It will be
a great delight for him.   He has asked after you
several times to-day.   He is impatient to see you.
[*She turns to* LORENZO GADDI.]   To-morrow, then.

> [*She goes out with a light and rapid step.   The
> sister, the* MAESTRO, *and the friend follow her
> with their eyes.*

FRANCESCA DONI.

[*With a kindly smile.*]   Poor Silvia !   For the last
few days, she seems as if she had wings.   When I
look at her sometimes, it seems to me as if she is
going to take flight towards happiness.   And no one
deserves happiness more ; is it not true, Maestro ?
You know her.

LORENZO GADDI.

Yes, she is really as your sisterly eyes see her.   She
comes winged out of her martyrdom.   There is a sort

of incessant quiver in her. I felt it just now, when
she stood near me. Truly she is in a state of grace.
There is no height to which she could not attain.
Lucio has in his hands a life of flame, an infinite
force.

FRANCESCA DONI.

You were with him some time to-day.

LORENZO GADDI.

Yes, hours.

FRANCESCA DONI.

How was he ?

LORENZO GADDI.

Running over with sweetness, and a little be-
wildered. You will see him presently, Dalbo. His
sensitiveness is a danger. Those who love him can
do him much good and much harm. A word agitates
and convulses him. Watch over all your words, you
who love him. Good-bye. I must go.

[*Takes leave of them both.*
FRANCESCA DONI.

Good-bye, Maestro. Perhaps we shall see you here
again to-morrow. I hope so. You have a horror of
my stairs !

[*She accompanies the old man to the door ; then
returns to the friend.*

What a fire of intelligence and of goodness, in that

B

old man ! When he comes into a room he seems to
bring comfort to all. The sad rejoice and the merry
become fervent.

COSIMO DALBO.

He inspires the soul ; he belongs to the noblest
race of mankind. His work is a continual exaltation
of life; it is the continual force of communicating a
spark, whether to his statues or to the creatures whom
he meets by the way. Lorenzo Gaddi seems to me to
deserve a far higher fame than he receives from his
contempories.

FRANCESCA DONI.

It is true, it is true. If you knew what energy
and what delicacy he showed, in that horrible affair !
When the thing happened, my sister was not there ;
she was with our mother, at Pisa, with Beata. The
thing happened in the studio, there, on the Mugnone,
in the evening. Only the caretaker heard the report.
When he discovered the truth, he ran to tell Lorenzo
Gaddi before any one else. In the anguish and
horror of that winter evening, in the midst of all the
confusion and uncertainty, he alone never lost his
presence of mind, nor had a single instant's hesitation.
He preserved a strange lucidity, by which every one
was dominated. He made every arrangement: all
obeyed him. It was he who had poor Lucio brought

to the house here, half dead. The doctor despaired of
saving him. He alone declared, with an obstinate
faith : " No, he will not die, he will not die, he cannot
die." I believed him. Ah, what a heroic night,
Dalbo. And then the arrival of Silvia, his telling
her himself, forbidding her to enter the room where
a mere breath might have quenched that glimmer of
life : and her strength, her incredible endurance
under watching and waiting for whole weeks, the
proud and silent vigilance with which she guarded
the threshold as if to hinder the coming of death !

Cosimo Dalbo.

And I was far away, unconscious of all, blissfully
idle in a boat on the Nile ! Yet I had a kind of pre-
sentiment, before leaving. That was why I tried
every means to persuade Lucio to go with me, as
we had often dreamed of doing together. He had
then finished his statue ; and I thought that his
liberty was in that wonderful marble. He said,
" Not yet ! " And a few months after he was
seeking it in death. Ah, if I had not gone away, if
I had stayed by him, if I had been more faithful, if I
had known how to defend him against the enemy,
nothing would have happened.

FRANCESCA DONI.

There is nothing to regret if so much good can come out of so much evil. Who knows in what sadness of despair my sister might have perished, if the violence of that act had not suddenly reunited her to Lucio ! But do not think that the enemy has laid down arms. She has not abandoned the field.

COSIMO DALBO.

Who ? Gioconda Dianti ?

FRANCESCA DONI.

[*Motioning to him to be silent, and lowering her voice.*] Do not say that name !

SCENE III.

LUCIO SETTALA *appears on the threshold of the door, leaning on the arm of* SILVIA ; *he is pale and thin, and his eyes look extraordinarily large with suffering ; a faint, sweet smile gives refinement to a voluptuous mouth.*

LUCIO SETTALA.

Cosimo !

Cosimo Dalbo.

[*Turning and running up to him.*] Oh, Lucio, dear, dear friend!

> [*He puts his arms about the convalescent, while Silvia moves aside, nearer to her sister, and goes out with her, slowly, pausing for a moment to look at her husband before going.*

You are well again, are you not? You are not suffering now? I find you a little pale, a little thin, but not so very much. You look as I have seen you sometimes after a period of feverish work, when you have been with your clay for twelve hours a day, consumed with that fire. Do you remember?

Lucio Settala.

[*Looking confusedly about him, to see if Silvia is still in the room.*] Yes, yes.

Cosimo Dalbo.

Then too your eyes looked larger. . . .

Lucio Settala.

[*With an indefinable, almost childish restlessness.*] And Silvia? Where is Silvia gone? Wasn't she here with Francesca?

COSIMO DALBO.

They have left us alone.

LUCIO SETTALA.

Why? She thinks, perhaps. . ·. . No, I have
nothing to tell you, I know nothing now any more.
Perhaps you know. For me, no; I don't remember.
I don't want to remember. Tell me about yourself!
Tell me about yourself! Is the desert beautiful?

> [*He speaks in a singular way, as if in a dream,
> with a mixture of agitation and stupor.*

COSIMO DALBO.

I will tell you. But you must not tire yourself.
I will tell you all my pilgrimage; I will come here
every day, if I may; I will stay with you as long as
you like, only not long enough to tire you. Sit here.

LUCIO SETTALA.

[*Smiling.*] Do you think I am so feeble?

COSIMO DALBO.

No, you are all right now, but it is better for you
not to tire yourself. Sit here.

> [*He makes him sit down near the window, and
> looks out at the hill clearly outlined against
> the April sky.*

Ah, my dear friend, I have seen marvellous things with these eyes, and they have drunk light in comparison with which this seems ashen ; but, when I see again a simple line like that (look at San Miniato !) I seem to find myself again, after an interval of wandering. Look at that dear hill ! The pyramid of Cheops does not make one forget the Bella Villanella ; and more than once, in the gardens of Koubbeh and Gizeh, hives of honey, chewing a grain of resin, I thought of a slim Tuscan cypress on the edge of a narrow grove of olives.

Lucio Settala.

[*Half closing his eyelids under the breath of Spring.*] It is good to be here, is it not ? There is an odour of violets. Perhaps there is a bunch of violets in the room. Silvia puts them everywhere, even under my pillow.

Cosimo Dalbo.

Do you know, I have brought you the violets of the desert, between the pages of a Koran. I gathered them in the garden of a Persian monastery, near the Thebaid, on the side of the Mokattam, on an eminence of sand. There, in a cavern dug out of the mountain, covered with carpets and cushions, the

monks offer their visitors a tea with a special flavour,
Arab tea, perfumed with violets.

Lucio Settala.

And you have brought them for me, buried in a
book! How happy you were to be able to gather
them, so far away; and I might have been with you.

Cosimo Dalbo.

There, all was oblivion. I went up by a long,
straight stone staircase, that leads from the foot of
the mountain to the gate of the Bectaschiti. The
desert was all about; vast, hallucinating dryness, in
which there was no life but the stirring of wind and
the quivering of heat. I could only distinguish here
and there, between the sand-heaps, the white stones
of Arab cemeteries. I heard the crying of hawks
high up in the sky. I saw on the Nile multitudes of
boats with great lateen sails, white, slow, going on,
going on, like snow-flakes. And little by little I was
caught up into an ecstasy that you can never have
known, the ecstasy of light.

Lucio Settala.

[*In a far off voice.*] And I might have been with
you, loitering, forgetting, dreaming, drunk with light.
You went down the Nile, did you not? in an ancient

boat loaded with wine-skins, sacks, and cages. You landed on an island towards evening; you were dressed in white serge; you were thirsty; you drank at a spring; you walked barefoot upon flowers; and the odour was so strong that you seemed to have forgotten hunger. Ah, I thought, I felt, these things from my pillow. And I followed you through the desert, when the fever was at its height; through a desert of red sand, sown with glittering stones that splintered crackling like twigs in the fire.

A pause. He leans forward a little, saying in a clear voice and with open eyes:
And the Sphinx?

Cosimo Dalbo.

I saw it first at night, by the light of stars, sunken into the sand that still keeps the violent imprint of whirlwinds. The face and the croup rose out of that quieted storm, all that was human and all that was bestial in it. The face, whose mutilations were hidden by the shadow, seemed to me at that moment exquisitely beautiful : calm, august, cerulean as the night, almost meek. There is nothing in the world, Lucio, so much alone as that ; but my mind was, as it were, before multitudes who had slept, and on whose eyelashes the dew had fallen. Then I saw it

again by day. The face was bestial, like the croup;
the nose and throat were eaten away; the droppings
of birds fouled the fillets. It was the heavy wingless
monster imagined by the excavators of tombs, by the
embalmers of corpses. And I saw, in the sun before
me, your Sphinx, pure and imperious, with wings
imprisoned alive in the shoulders.

LUCIO SETTALA.

[*With a sudden emtion.*] My statue ?   You mean my
statue ?   You saw it, ah, yes, before you went; and
you found it beautiful.

> [*He looks uneasily towards the door, fearing*
> SILVIA *might hear him, and lowers his voice.*

You found it beautiful ?

COSIMO DALBO.

Exquisitely beautiful.

> [LUCIO *covers his eyes with both hands and*
> *remains for some seconds as if trying to evoke*
> *a vision in the darkness.*

LUCIO SETTALA.

[*Uncovering his eyes.*] I no longer see it. It escapes
me. It comes and goes in a breath, confusedly. If I
had it here before me now it would seem new to me:

I should cry out. And yet I carved it, with these hands!

[*He looks at his thin, sensitive hands. His agitation increases.*

I don't know. I don't know. In the beginning of my fever, when I still had the bullet in my flesh, and the continual murmuring of death in my lost soul, I saw it standing at the foot of the bed, lit like a torch, as if I myself had moulded it out of some incandescent material. So for many days and nights I saw it through my eyelids, It grew brighter as my fever increased. When my pulse burned it turned to flame. It was as if all the blood shed at its feet had gone up it into and boiled up in it . . .

COSIMO DALBO.

[*Uneasily, looking towards the door, with the same fear.*] Lucio, Lucio, you said just now that you knew nothing now, that you did not want to remember anything. Lucio!

[*He gently shakes his friend, who remains rigid.*

LUCIO SETTALA.

[*Recollecting himself.*] Do not. fear. I have left it all far, far behind me, at the bottom of the sea. The statue was drowned too, with all the rest, after the shipwreck. That is why I can no longer see it except confusedly, as if through deep water.

Cosimo Dalbo.

It alone shall be saved, to live for ever; and so much sorrow shall not have been suffered in vain, so much evil shall not have been useless, if one thing so beautiful remains over, to be added to the ornament of life.

Lucio Settala.

[*Smiling again with his faint smile and speaking in his far-off voice.*] It is true. I sometimes think of the fate of one whose ship and all that was in it went down in a storm. On a day as calm as this, he took a boat and a net, and he returned to the place of the shipwreck, hoping to draw something up out of the depths. And, after much labour, he drew on shore a statue. And the statue was so beautiful that he wept for joy to see it again; and he sat down on the sea-shore to gaze upon it, and was content with that gain, and would seek after nothing more: "well, I forget the rest !" [*He rises hastily.*

Why has not Silvia come back ? [*He listens.*

Who is laughing? Ah, it is Beata in the garden. Look; San Miniato is all gold; it lightens. Is there a more glorious light at Thebes ?

Cosimo Dalbo.

The ecstasy of light! I told you : you can know it
nowhere else. Circles, garlands, wheels, roses of
splendour, innumerable sparkles. . . . The verses of
the *Paradiso* recur to one's mind. Only Dante has
found dazzling words. In certain hours the Nile
becomes the flood of topazes, the "marvellous gulf."
Like a stone in water, a gesture in the air arouses
thousands and thousands of waves. All things swim
in light; all the leaves drip with it. The women,
who pass along the stream with full wine-skins,
actually flame like the angelic host in the song, " dis-
tinct in light and form."

> [Lucio, *catching sight of a bunch of violets on the
> table, takes them up and buries his face in
> them, to drink in their odour.*

Lucio Settala.

[*Still holding the violets to his nostrils and half-
closing his eyes with delight.*] Are the women of the
Nile beautiful ?

Cosimo Dalbo.

Some, in youth, have bodies of marvellous purity
and elegance. You, who like firm and active muscles,
a certain acerbity in form, long, nervous legs, would

find incomparable models there. How often have I thought of you! In the island of Elephantina I had a little friend of fourteen; a girl golden as a date, thin, lithe, firm, with strong, arched loins, straight, strong legs, perfect knees; a very rare thing, as you know. In all that hard slenderness, which gave one the impression of a javelin, sharp and precise, three things delighted me with their infinitely soft grace : the mouth, the shadow of the eyelashes, the tips of the fingers. She braided her hair with fingers rosy-tipped like petals dyed with purple : and to watch her in that act, on the threshold of her white house, was the delight of my mornings. I should like to have taken her away with the statuettes, the scarabæi, the cloths, the tobacco, the scents, the weapons. I have brought you a beautiful bow that I bought at Assouan, and that is a little like her.

LUCIO SETTALA.

[*With a slight perturbation, throwing back his head.*] She must have been a delicious creature !

COSIMO DALBO.

Delicious and harmless. She was like a beautiful bow, but her arrows were without venom.

LUCIO SETTALA.

You loved her ?

COSIMO DALBO.

As I love my horse and my dogs.

LUCIO SETTALA.

Ah, you were happy there; your life was light and
easy. It must have been the island of Elephantina
where I saw you come on shore, in a dream. I might
have been with you! But I will go, I will leave here.
Do you not long to return ? I will have a white
house on the Nile; I will make my statues with the
slime of the river, and set them up in that light of
yours that will turn them to gold for me. Silvia!
Silvia!

[*He calls towards the door as if seized by a
sudden impatience, an anxious will to live.*
Would it be too late ?

COSIMO DALBO.

It is too late. The great heats are coming on.

LUCIO SETTALA.

What does it matter ? I love summer heat, sultri-
ness even. All the pomegranates will be in flower in
the gardens, and when it rains they will see those

large, warm drops that make the earth sigh for
pleasure.

Cosimo Dalbo.

But the Khamsin? when all the desert rises up
against the sun?

> [Silvia *appears on the threshold, smiling, her
> whole being visibly animated. She has
> changed her gown ; she is dressed in a clearer,
> more spring-like colour ; and she carries in
> her hands a bunch of fresh roses.*

Silvia Settala.

What do you say, Dalbo, against the sun? Did
you call, Lucio?

Lucio Settala.

[*Re-taken by a kind of restless timidity, as of a man
who feels the need of self-abandonment, to which he
dares not give way.*] Yes, I called you, because I
thought you were never coming back. Cosimo was
telling me of so many beautiful things. I wanted you
to hear them too.

> [*He looks at his wife with surprise in his eyes, as
> if he discovered a new charm in her.*

Were you going out?

Silvia Settala.

[*Blushing slightly.*] Ah, you are looking at my gown.

I put it on to see how it looked, while Francesca was
there. My sister sends her apologies to you both for
having gone without coming to say good-bye. She
was in a hurry: her children were waiting for her.
She hopes, Dalbo, that you will come and see her
soon. [*She puts the roses on a table.*
Will you dine with us to-night?

COSIMO DALBO.

Thanks. I cannot to-night. My mother expects
me.

SILVIA SETTALA.

Naturally. To-morrow, then?

COSIMO DALBO.

To-morrow. I will bring my presents for you,
Lucio.

LUCIO SETTALA.

[*With childish curiosity.*] Yes, yes, bring them, bring
them.

SILVIA SETTALA.

[*Smiling mysteriously.*] I too am to have a present
to-morrow.

LUCIO SETTALA.

From whom?

SILVIA SETTALA.

From the Maestro.

C

LUCIO SETTALA.

What ?

SILVIA SETTALA.

You shall see.

LUCIO SETTALA.

[*With a joyous movement.*] You too shall see all the beautiful things that Cosimo has brought me : cloths, scents, weapons, scarabæi. . . .

COSIMO DALBO.

Amulets against every evil, talismans for happiness. On Gebel-el-Tair, in a Coptic convent, I found the most powerful of scarabæi. The monk told me a long story of a cenobite who, at the time of the first persecution, took refuge in a vault, and found a mummy there, and took it out of its swathings of balm, and restored it to life, and the resuscitated mummy, with its painted lips, told him the story of its old life, which had been one whole tissue of happiness. In the end, as the cenobite wished to convert it, it preferred to lie down again in its embalmings ; but first it gave him the guardian scarabæus. To tell you what use was made of it by the solitary, and through what vicissitudes it passed across the centuries into the hands of the good Copt, would take too long. Certainly, a

more powerful one is not in all Egypt. Here it is: I
offer it to you, I offer it to you both.

> [*He hands the amulet to* Silvia, *who examines it
> carefully and then passes it to* Lucio, *with a
> sudden light in her eyes.*

Silvia Settala.

How blue it is   It is brighter than a turquoise.
Look.

Cosimo Dalbo.

The Copt said to me: " Small as a gem great as a
destiny ! "

> [Lucio *turns the mystic stone between his fingers,
> which tremble a little, fumblingly.*

Good-bye then: to-morrow! Good night.

Silvia Settala.

[*Picking a rose out of the bunch and offering it to
him.*] Here is a fresh rose in exchange for the
amulet. Take it to your mother

Cosimo Dalbo.

Thanks. To-morrow ! [*He salutes them again and
goes out.*

SCENE IV.

LUCIO SETTALA *smiles timidly, turning the scarabæus*
between his fingers, while SILVIA *puts the roses*
in a vase. Both, in the silence, hear the beating
of their anxious hearts. The setting sun gilds
the room. In the square of the window is seen
the pallid sky; San Miniato shines on the
height; the air is soft, without a breath of
wind.

LUCIO SETTALA.

[*Looking into the air, and listening anxiously.*]
There is a bee in the room.

SILVIA SETTALA.

Raising her head.]   A bee?

LUCIO SETTALA.

Yes.   Don't you hear it ?

[*Both listen to the murmur.*

SILVIA SETTALA.

You are right.

LUCIO SETTALA.

Perhaps you brought it in with the roses.

Silvia Settala.

Beata picked these.

Lucia Settala.

I heard her laughing, just now, down in the
garden.

Silvia Settala.

How pleased she is to be home again!

Lucio Settala.

was a good thing to send her away then.

Silvia Settala.

She is stronger and lovelier for having breathed
the odour of the pines. How good the spring must
be at Bocca d'Arno! Would you not like to
there for a while?

Lucio Settala.

There, by the sea. . . . Would you like it?
[*Their voices are altered by a slight tremor.*

Silvia Settala.

It has always been a dream of mine to pass one
spring there.

LUCIO SETTALA.

[*Choked with emotion.*] Your dream is mine,
Silvia.   [*The amulet falls from his hands.*

SILVIA SETTALA.

[*Stooping quickly to pick it up.*] Ah, you have let
it fall! They would say it is a bad omen. See.
I put it on Beata's head. "Small as a gem, great as
a destiny!"
    [*She lays the amulet delicately upon the roses.*

LUCIO SETTALA.

[*Holding out his hands to her, as if imploring.*]
Silvia! Silvia!

SILVIA SETTALA.

[*Running to him*] Do you feel ill? You look
paler. Ah, you have tired yourself too much to-day,
you are worn out. Sit here, come. Will you sip
some of this cordial? Do you feel as if you are
going to faint? Tell me!

LUCIO SETTALA.

[*Taking her hands with an outburst of love.*] No, no,
Silvia; I never felt so well. You, you sit down, sit
here; and I at your feet, at last, with all my soul, to
adore you, to adore you!

[She sinks back on the divan and he falls on his knees before her. She is convulsed and trembling, and lays her hand on his lips, as if to keep him from speaking. Breath and words pass between her fingers.

At last! It was like a flood coming from far off, a flood of all the beautiful things and all the good things that you have poured out on my life since you began to love me; and my heart overflowed, ah, overflowed so that I staggered under the weight of it, and fainted and died of the pain and the sweetness of it, because I dared not say. . . .

SILVIA SETTALA.

[Her face white, her voice almost extinct.] No more say no more!

LUCIO SETTALA.

Hear me, hear me! All the sorrows that you have suffered, the wounds that you have received without a cry, the tears that you have hidden lest I should have shame and remorse, the smiles with which you have veiled your agonies, your infinite pity for my wanderings, your invincible courage in the face of death, your hard fight for my life, your hope always alight beside my bed, your watches, cares, continual tremors, expectation, silence, joy, all that is deep, all

that is sweet and heroic in you, I know it all, I feel
it all, dear soul ; and, if violence is enough to break
a yoke, if blood is enough for redemption (oh, let
me speak!) I bless the evening and the hour that
brought me dying into this house of your martyrdom
and of your faith to receive once more at your hands,
these divine hands that tremble, the gift of life.

> [*He presses his convulsed mouth against the
> palms of her hands, aad she gazes at him
> through the tears that moisten her eyelids,
> transfigured with unexpected happiness.*

SILVIA SETTALA.

[*In a faint and broken voice.*] No more, say no
more ! My heart cannot bear it. You suffocate me
with joy. I longed for one word from you, only one,
no more ; and all at once you flood me with love, you
fill up every vein, you raise me to the other side of
hope, you outpass my dreams, you give me happiness
beyond all expectation. Ah, what did you say of my
sorrows ? What is sorrow endured, what is silence
constrained, what is a tear, what is a smile, now, in
the face of this flood that bears me away ? I feel as
if by-and-by, for you, for you, I shall be sorry not to
have suffered more. Perhaps I have not reached the

depths of sorrow, but I know that I have reached the height of happiness.

> [*She blindly caresses his head, as it lies on her knees.*

Rise, rise! Come nearer to my heart, rest on me, give way to my tenderness, press my hands on your eyelids, be silent, dream, call back the deep forces of your life. Ah, it is not me alone that you must love, not me alone, but the love I have for you : love my love! I am not beautiful, I am not worthy of your eyes, I am a humble creature in the shadow ; but my love is wonderful, it is on high, on high, it is alone, it is sure as the day, it is stronger than death, it can work miracles ; it shall give you all that you ask. You can ask more than you have ever hoped.

> [*She draws him to her heart, raising his head. His eyes are closed, his lips tight set, he is as pale as death, drunk and exhausted with emotion.*

Rise, rise! Come nearer to my heart ; rest on me. Do you not feel that you can give yourself up to me that nothing in the world is surer than my breast ? that you can find it always ? Ah, I have sometimes thought that this certitude might intoxicate you like glory.

> [*He kneels before her with uplifted face ; she with*

both hands pushes back the hair to uncover his
whole forehead.

Beautiful, strong forehead, sealed and blessed !
May all the germs of spring awaken in your new
thoughts !

> [*Trembling she presses her lips to his forehead.*
> *Silently he stretches out his arms towards the*
> *suppliant. The sunset is like a dawn.*

END OF THE FIRST ACT.

THE SECOND ACT

The same room, the same hour of the day. A cloudy and changing sky is seen through the window.

SCENE I

COSIMO DALBO *is seated by a table, on which he rests his elbows, putting his hand to his forehead, grave and thoughtful.* LUCIO SETTALA *is on foot, restless and agitated ; he moves about the room uncertainly, giving way to the anguish that oppresses him.*

LUCIO SETTALA.

Yes, I am going to tell you. Why should I hide the truth ? From you ! I have had a letter, I have opened it, read it.

COSIMO DALBO

From Gioconda ?

LUCIO SETTALA.

From her.

COSIMO DALBO.

A love letter ?

LUCIO SETTALA.

It burnt my fingers.

COSIMO DALBO.

Well ?

[*He hesitates. In a voice changed by emotion.*
You still love her ?

LUCIO SETTALA.

[*With a shudder of dread.*] No, no, no.

COSIMO DALBO.

[*Looking into the depths of his eyes.*] You no longer
love her ?

LUCIO SETTALA.

[*Entreatingly.*] Oh, do not torture me.   I suffer.

COSIMO DALBO.

But what is it then that distresses you ?   [*A pause.*

LUCIO SETTALA.

Every day, at an hour that I know, she waits for
me, there, at the foot of the statue, alone.

[*Another pause. The two men seem as if they*

saw before them something strong and living,
a Will, evoked by those brief words.

COSIMO DALBO.

She waits for you? Where? In your studio?
How could she get in?

LUCIO SETTALA.

She has a key : the key of that time.

COSIMO DALBO.

She waits for you! She thinks, she desires, then,
that you should still belong to her?

LUCIO SETTALA.

You have said it.

COSIMO DALBO.

And what shall you do?

LUCIO SETTALA.

What shall I do? [*A pause.*

COSIMO DALBO.

You vibrate like a flame.

LUCIO SETTALA.

I suffer.

COSIMO DALBO.

You are burning.

LUCIO SETTALA.

[*Vehemently.*] No.

COSIMO DALBO.

Listen. She is terrible. One cannot fight against her save at a distance. That is why I wanted to take you with me, across the sea. You preferred death to the sea. Another (you know who, and your heart bleeds for her) has saved you from death. And now you can live only for her.

LUCIO SETTALA

It is true.

COSIMO DALBO.

You must go away, fly from her.

LUCIO SETTALA.

For always?

COSIMO DALBO.

For some time

LUCIO SETTALA.

She will wait for me.

COSIMO DALBO.

You will be stronger.

LUCIO SETTALA.

Her power will have increased. She will have
more profoundly impregnated with herself the place
that is dear to me for the work's sake that was
achieved there. I shall see her from far off, like the
guardian of a statue into which I put the most vivid
breath of my soul.

COSIMO DALBO.

You love her.

LUCIO SETTALA.

[*Despairingly.*] No. I do not love her. But
think : she will always be the stronger : she knows
what conquers and what binds me ; she is armed
with a fascination from which I cannot free my soul
except by tearing her out of my heart. Must I try
again ?

COSIMO DALBO.

Ah, you are raving !

LUCIO SETTALA.

The place where I have dreamed, where I have
worked, where I have wept with joy, where I have
cried on glory, where I have seen death, is her
conquest. She knows that I cannot keep away from
it or renounce it, that the most precious part of my

GIOCONDA

substance is diffused there : and she waits for me, certain.

COSIMO DALBO.

Does she then exercise an inviolable right there ? Can no one forbid her entrance ?

LUCIO SETTALA.

[*With a profound emotion.*] Turn her out ?

COSIMO DALBO.

No : but there may be another way, less hard, the simplest way : ask her for the key which she has no right to retain.

LUCIO SETTALA.

And who is to ask her for it ?

COSIMO DALBO.

Any one of us, I myself, respectfully, in the name of necessity.

LUCIO SETTALA.

She would refuse, she would look upon you as a stranger.

COSIMO DALBO.

You yourself then.

LUCIO SETTALA.

I ? I face her ?

COSIMO DALBO.

No, write to her. [*A pause.*

LUCIO SETTALA.

[*With the accent of absolute impossibility.*] I cannot.
And it would all be in vain.

COSIMO DALBO.

But there is another way : leave that house, clear
out everything, take everything somewhere else.
You will thus avoid the intolerable sadness of
memory. How is it you do not realise that change
is necessary, if your life is to renew itself, so that the
companion you have found again may help you in
your work? Would you have her sit where the
other had been? Would you have her always see
before her eyes the vision of that horrible evening?

LUCIO SETTALA.

[*Smiling, disheartened and bitter.*] Well, yes, you
are right : we will leave here, we will go somewhere
else, we will choose a beautiful solitary place, we will
shake off the dust from old things, open all the
windows, let in the pure air, take a heap of clay a
block of marble, set up a monument to liberty.

D

[*He breaks off. His voice becomes singularly
    calm.*

One morning, Gioconda will knock at the new door;
I shall open to her: she will come in: without
surprise I shall say to her, " Welcome."
                        [*Unable to restrain his bitterness.*
Ah, but you are like a child ! The whole thing seems
to you no more than a key. Call in a locksmith,
change the lock, and I am saved.

COSIMO DALBO.

[*Tenderly and sadly.*] Do not be angry. At first I
thought you had simply to rid yourself of an intruder.
Now I see that my advice was childish.

LUCIO SETTALA.

[*Imploringly.*] Cosimo, my friend, do understand
me !

COSIMO DALBO.

understand, but you deny it.

LUCIO SETTALA.

[*Again carried away by excitement.*] I deny
nothing. I deny nothing. Would you have me cry
to you that I love her ?
                        [*Looks about him in an aimless bewilderment.*

[*Passes his hand across his forehead with an
air of suffering. Lowers his voice.*

You should have let me die. Think, if I who was
intoxicated with life, if I who was frantic with strength
and pride, if I wanted to die, be sure I knew there
was an insuperable necessity for it. Not being able to
live either with or without her, I resolved to quit the
world. Think: I who looked on the world as my
garden, and had every lust after every beauty! Be
sure, then, I knew there was an insuperable necessity,
an iron destiny. You should have let me die.

COSIMO DALBO.

You have forgotten the divine miracle, cruelly.

LUCIO SETTALA.

I am not cruel. Because I was in horror of that
cruelty towards which the violence of evil drew me,
because I would not trample upon a more than human
virtue, because I could not endure the sweetness of a
little unconscious voice questioning me, because I
wished to keep myself from the worst of all (do you
understand?) I made my resolve. And because I am
in horror of beginning over again, therefore I hate
myself; because to-day I am like one who has taken
a narcotic in despair, and who wakes up again, after a

sound sleep, and finds the same old despair by his bedside.

Cosimo Dalbo.

The same! And your first words are still in my ears: " I know nothing now, I don't remember, I don't want to remember any more." You seemed as if you had forgotten all, as if you reached out after some new good thing. The sound of your voice is still in my ears as you called to Beata's mother, getting up hurriedly, impatient, as if with an ardour that permits no delay. I still see the way you looked at her, when she entered, tremulous as hope. And, surely, that night you must needs have knelt to her, and she must have wept over you, and both together must have felt the goodness of life.

Lucio Settala.

Yes, yes, it was indeed so: adoration! All my soul was prostrate at her feet, knowing all that is divine in her, with an intoxication of humility, with a fervour of unspeakable gratitude. I was carried away. You spoke of the ecstasy of light: I experienced it in that moment. Every stain was wiped out, every shadow cleared away. Life had a new splendour. I thought I was saved for ever.   [*He breaks off.*

COSIMO DALBO.

But then?

LUCIO SETTALA.

Then I knew that there was something else that must be abolished in me: the force that flows incessantly to my fingers, as if to reproduce

COSIMO DALBO.

What do you mean?

LUCIO SETTALA.

I mean that I should perhaps have been saved, if I had forgotten art also. Those days, there in my bed, as I looked at my feeble hands, it seemed to me incredible that I should ever create again ; it seemed to me as if I had lost all my power. I felt completely estranged from the world of form in which I had lived . . . *before I died.* I thought: " Lucio Settala, the sculptor, is dead." And I dreamt of becoming the gardener of a little garden.

> [*He sits down, as if quieted, half closing his eyes,
> with a weary air, a scarcely visible smile of
> irony.*

To prune roses, water them, pick the caterpillars off them, clip the box with shears, train the ivy up the walls, in a little garden sloping to the waters of oblivion ; and not regret that one has left on the other shore a glorious park, populous with laurels, and cypresses, and myrtles, and marbles, and dreams. You see me there, happy, with shining shears, dressed in twill.

Cosimo Dalbo.

I do not see you.

Lucio Settala.

It is a pity, my friend.

Cosimo Dalbo.

But who forbids your return to the great park ? You can return to it by the alley of cypresses, and find your tutelar genius at the end of the way.

Lucio Settala.

[*Leaping to his feet, like one who again loses self-control.*] Tutelar ! Ah, you seem to heap one word on another, like bandages on lint, for fear of feeling the pulsation of life. Have you ever put your finger on an open artery, a torn tendon ?

Cosimo Dalbo.

Lucio, your anger grows on you every minute. You have something wry and acrid, a kind of ex-asperation which hinders you from being just. You

are not yet out of convalescence, you are not yet well.
A sudden shock has come to disturb the placid work
that nature was carrying out in you. Your new-born
strength festers. If my advice were worth anything,
I would bid you go at once to Bocca d'Arno, as you
proposed. There, between the woods and the sea, you
will find once more a little calm, and you will think
over what your attitude must be ; and you will find
too the goodness that will give you light.

LUCIO SETTALA.

Goodness! goodness! Do you think then that
light must come from goodness and not from that
profound instinct which turns and hurries my spirit
towards the most glorious images of life ? I was
born to make statues. When a material form has
gone out of my hands with the imprint of beauty,
the office assigned to me by nature is fulfilled. I
have not exceeded my own law, whether or not I
have exceeded the laws of right.. Is it not really
true ? Do you admit it ?

COSIMO DALBO.

Proceed.

LUCIO SETTALA.

[*Lowering his voice.*] The sport of illusion has
mated me with a creature who was never meant for

me. She is a soul of inestimable price, before whom I kneel and worship. But I am not a sculptor of souls. She was not meant for me. When the other appeared before me, I thought of all the blocks of marble hidden in the caves of far mountains, that I might arrest in each of them one of her motions.

Cosimo Dalbo.

But now you have obeyed the commandment of Nature, in creating your masterpiece. When I saw your statue I thought that you were free from her. You have perpetuated a frail sample of the species in an ideal and indestructible type. Are you not therefore satisfied ?

Lucio Settala.

[*More excitedly.*] A thousand statues, not one ! She is always diverse, like a cloud that from instant to instant seems changed without your seeing it change. Every motion of her body destroys one harmony and creates another yet more beautiful. You implore her to stay, to remain motionless ; and across all her immobility there passes a torrent of obscure forces, as thoughts pass in the eyes. Do you understand ? do you understand ? The life of the eyes is the look, that indefinable thing, more expressive than any word, than any sound, infinitely deep

and yet instantaneous as a breath, swifter than a
flash, innumerable, omnipotent : in a word, *the
look*. Now imagine the life of the look diffused
over all her body. Do you understand ? The quiver
of an eyelid transfigures a human face and expresses
an immensity of joy or sorrow. · The eyelashes of the
creature whom you love are lowered : the shadow
encircles you as the waters encircle an island : they are
raised : the flame of summer burns up the world.
Another quiver : your soul dissolves like a drop of
water; another: you are lord of the universe. Imagine
that mystery over all her body! Imagine through
all her limbs, from the forehead to the sole of the
foot, that flash of lightning, like life ! Can one chisel
the look ? The ancients made their statues blind.
Now, imagine, her whole body is like the look.

> [*A pause. He looks about him suspiciously,
> in fear of being heard. He comes nearer
> to his friend, who listens with increasing
> emotion.*

I have told you : a thousand statues, not one. Her
beauty lives in every block of marble. I felt this,
with an anxiety made up of regret and fervour, one
day at Carrara, when she was with me, and we saw,
coming down the mountain-side, those great oxen with
yokes, drawing the marble in waggons. An aspect of

her perfection was enclosed for me in each of those
formless masses. It seemed to me as if there went out
from her towards the raw material a thousand life-
giving sparks, as from a shaken torch. We had to
choose a block. I remember, it was a calm day. The
marble shone in the sun like the eternal snows. We
heard from time to time the rumbling of the mines
that tore asunder the bowels of the silent mountain.
I shall never forget that hour, though I were to die
over again. She went into the midst of that concourse
of white cubes, stopping before each. She leant over,
observed the grain attentively, seemed to explore the
inner veins, hesitated, smiled, passed on. To my eyes
her garments were no covering. There was a sort of
divine affinity between her flesh and the marble that
she leant over until her breath touched it. A confused aspiration seemed to rise to her from that inert
whiteness. The wind, the sun, the grandeur of the
mountains, the long lines of yoked oxen, and the
ancient curve of the yokes, and the creaking of the
waggons, and the cloud that rose from the Tirreno,
and the lofty flight of an eagle, everything I saw
exalted my spirit into a limitless poetry, intoxicated
with a dream that I had never equalled. Ah,
Cosimo, Cosimo, I have dared to throw away a life on
which there gleams the glory of such a memory.

When she laid her hand on the marble that she had
chosen, and turning to me said " This," all the mountains, from root to summit, breathed beauty.

> [*An extraordinary fervour warms his voice and
> quickens his gestures. The listener is carried
> away by it, and makes no sign.*

Ah, now you understand ! You will never ask me
again if I am satisfied. Now you know how furious
must be my impatience when I think that she is
there now, alone, at the foot of the Sphinx, awaiting
me. Think, the statue rises above her, immobile,
immutable, in its immunity from all sorrow ; and she
is there, grieving, and her life is ebbing away, and
something of her perishes continually. Delay is death,
But you do not know, you do not know. . . .

> [*He speaks as if about to confide a secret.*

COSIMO DALBO.

What

LUCIO SETTALA.

You do not know that I had begun another
statue ?

COSIMO DALBO.

Another ?

LUCIO SETTALA.

Yes, it was left unfinished, sketched out in the
clay. If the clay dries, all is lost.

Cosimo Dalbo.

Well ?

Lucio Settala.

I thought it was lost.

> [*An irresistible smile shines in his eyes. His*
> *voice trembles.*

It is not lost ; it still lives. The last touch of the thumb is there, still living.

> [*He makes the gesture of moulding, instinctively.*

Cosimo Dalbo

How ?

Lucio Settala.

She knows the ways of the art, she knows how the clay is kept soft   Once she used to help me. She herself damped the cloths

Cosimo Dalbo.

So she thought of keeping the clay moist while you were dying !

Lucio Settala.

Was not that too a way of opposing death ? Was not that too an act of faith, admirable ? She preserved my work.

Cosimo Dalbo.

While the other preserved your life.

LUCIO SETTALA.

[*Gloomily, lowering his forehead, without looking at his friend, in an almost hard voice.*] Which of the two is worth more? Life is intolerable to me, if it was only given back with such a dragging weight on it. I have told you: you should have let me die. What greater renunciation can I make than that I have made? Only death could stay the rush of desire that drives my whole being, fatally, towards its own particular good. Now I live again: I recognise in myself the same man, the same force. Who shall judge me if I follow out my destiny?

COSIMO DALBO.

[*Terrified, taking him by the arm as if to restrain him.*] But what will you do? Have you made up your mind?

[*Struck by the sudden terror in the voice and gesture of his friend,* LUCIO *hesitates.*

LUCIO SETTALA.

[*Putting his hands through his hair feverishly.*] What shall I do? What shall I do? Do you know a more cruel torture? I am dizzy; do you understand? If I think that she is there, and waiting for me, and the hours are passing, and my strength being lost, and my ardour burning itself away, dizziness clutches hold of my soul, and I am in fear that I shall be drawn there, perhaps to-night, perhaps to-morrow. Do you know what that dizziness is? Ah, if I could reopen the wound that they have closed for me!

Cosimo Dalbo.

[*Trying to lead him towards the window.*] Be calm, be calm, Lucio. Hush! I think I hear the voice. . .

Lucio Settala.

[*Starting.*] Silvia's? 		[*He turns deathly pale.*

Cosimo Dalbo.

Yes. Be calm. You are in a fever.

> [*He touches his forehead.* Lucio *leans on the window-sill, as if all his strength is leaving him.*

SCENE II.

Silvia Settala *enters with* Francesca Doni. *The latter has her arm round her sister's waist.*

Silvia Settala.

Oh, Dalbo, are you still here?

> [*She does not see* Lucio's *face, which he has turned to the open air.*

COSIMO DALBO.

[*Composing his countenance, and greeting* FRAN-
CESCA.] Lucio kept me.

SILVIA SETTALA.

Had he a great deal to tell you ?

COSIMO DALBO.

He always has a great deal to tell me, sometimes too
much.   And he is tired.

SILVIA SETTALA.

Did he tell you that we are going to Bocca d'Arno
on Saturday?

COSIMO DALBO.

Yes.   I know.

FRANCESCA DONI.

Have you ever been to Bocca d'Arno ?

COSIMO DALBO.

No, never.   I know the country about Pisa: San
Rossore, Gombo, San Pietro in Grado ; but I never
went as far as the mouth of the river.   I know that
the coast is most lovely.

[SILVIA *gazes fixedly at her husband, who remains
leaning motionless against the window-sill.*

FRANCESCA DONI.

Delicious at this time of the year : a low, open
coast, with fine sand : sea, river, and woods : the scent
of resin and sea-grass : sea-gulls, nightingales.   You
ought to come often and see Lucio while he is there.

COSIMO DALBO.
With pleasure.

SILVIA SETTALA.

We can put you up.
[*She leaves her sister and goes towards her
husband, with her light step.*

FRANCESCA DONI.

Our mother has a simple house there, but it is
large, white inside and outside, in a thicket of
oleanders and tamarinds, and there is an Empire
spinet, which used to belong—fancy to whom ?—to a
sister of Napoleon, the Duchess of Lucca, the terrible,
bony Elisa Baciocchi : a spinet that sometimes wakes
and weeps under Silvia's fingers ; and there is a boat,
if the Napoleonic relic doesn't tempt you, a lovely
boat, as white as the house.
[SILVIA *leans in silence against* LUCIO's *shoulder,
as if expectant.   He remains absorbed.*

COSIMO DALBO.

To live in a boat, on the water, aimlessly, there
is nothing so refreshing. I have lived like that for
weeks and weeks.

FRANCESCA DONI.

We ought to put our convalescent in a boat, and
confide him to the good sea.

SILVIA SETTALA.

[*Touching her husband lightly on the shoulder.*]
Lucio! [*He starts and turns.*] What are you doing ?
We are here. Here is Francesca.
    [*He looks his wife in the face, hesitatingly : then
    tries to smile.*

LUCIO SETTALA.

There is a shower coming. I was looking for the
first drops : the odour of the earth. . . .
    [*He turns again towards the window, and holds
    out his open hands : they tremble visibly.*

FRANCESCA DONI.

April either weeps or laughs.

E

LUCIO SETTALA.

Oh, Francesca, how are you?

FRANCESCA DONI.

Quite well.   And you, Lucio?

LUCIO SETTALA.

Quite well, quite well.

FRANCESCA DONI.

Are you going away on Saturday?

LUCIO SETTALA.

[*Looking at his wife, in a dreamy way.*] Where?

FRANCESCA DONI.

Why, to Bocca d'Arno.

LUCIO SETTALA.

Ah, yes, true.   My memory is quite gone.

SILVIA SETTALA.

Do you not feel well to-day?

LUCIO SETTALA.

Yes, yes, quite well.   The weather upsets me a
little ; but I feel well, pretty well.

[In the tone with which he pronounces these simple words there is an excess of dissimulalation, which gives him the strangeness of a madman. It is evident that the attention of the three bystanders is intolerable to him.

Are you going, Cosimo?

COSIMO DALBO.

Yes, I am going. It is time.

[He prepares to go.

LUCIO SETTALA.

I will go with you as far as the garden-gate.
[He leaves the window and goes towards the door, anxiously.

SILVIA SETTALA.

Are you going without your hat?

LUCIO SETTALA.

Yes, I am hot. Don't you feel how heavy the air is?

[He pauses on the threshold, waiting for his friend. A sharp pain suddenly goes through all hearts, striking every one silent.

COSIMO DALBO.

An revoir.

> [*He bows in a constrained way, and goes out
> with* LUCIO. SILVIA *bends her head, knitting
> her brows, as if she is thinking out some
> resolution. Then it seems as if she is lifted
> on a sudden wave of energy.*

FRANCESCA DONI.

Have you seen Gaddi ?

SILVIA SETTALA.

Not yet.   He has not come to-day.

FRANCESCA DONI.

Then you don't know.

SILVIA SETTALA.

What ?

FRANCESCA DONI.

What he has done ?

SILVIA SETTALA

No.

FRANCESCA DONI.

He went to see Dianti.

SILVIA SETTALA.

[*With restrained emotion.*] To see her ! When ?

FRANCESCA DONI.

Yesterday.

SILVIA SETTALA.

And you have seen him ?

FRANCESCA DONI.

Yes, I met him. He told me. . .

SILVIA SETTALA.

Speak, speak !

FRANCESCA DONI.

He went to see her yesterday, about three. He sent in his name. He was admitted at once. She received him smilingly, bowed, never said a word, stood before him, waiting for the old man to speak, listened to him quietly and respectfully. You can imagine what he might have said to persuade her to give back the key, to give up any further attempts, and not trouble a peace bought back at the price of blood, and what sorrow ! When he had finished she merely asked : " Did Lucio Settala send you to me ?" On his reply in the negative, she added very firmly : " Pardon me, but I cannot admit that any one but he has the right of asking what you have asked."

SILVIA SETTALA.

[*Turning pale and drawing herself up as if for a contest.*] Ah, that is her last word. Well, there is some one else who has an equal right and who will insist on her right. We shall see.

FRANCESCA DONI.

[*Startled.*] What are you thinking of doing, Silvia ?

SILVIA SETTALA.

What is necessary.

FRANCESCA DONI.

What then ?

SILVIA SETTALA.

Seeing her, facing her, in the place where she is an intruder. Do you understand ?

FRANCESCA DONI.

You would go there ?

SILVIA SETTALA

Yes, I am going there. I know her time. You yourself know it. I will wait for her. She shall see. We shall meet face to face at last.

FRANCESCA DONI.

You will not do it.

SILVIA SETTALA.

Why not ? Do you think I have not the courage ?

FRANCESCA DONI.

I entreat you, Silvia !

SILVIA SETTALA.

Do you think I tremble?

FRANCESCA DONI,

I entreat you !

SILVIA SETTALA.

Oh, be sure, I shall not lower my eyes, I shall not
faint. You ought to know me by now ; I have gone
through more than one ordeal.

FRANCESCA DONI.

I know, I know. Nothing is too much for you.
But think : to go there, after all that, in the very
place where the horrible thing happened, there, alone,
face to face with that woman, who has done you so
much injury.

Silvia Settala.

Well ? What of that ? Have I once—once, Francesca !—failed to accomplish what seemed to me
necessary ? Tell me, have you ever known me refuse
a burden ? From what torture have I drawn back ?
I have faced many other sorrows, as you know. You
are afraid that my heart will fail me if I set foot where
he fell ? But I had the courage then to look at him
through the crack of the door, when he lay on his bed
of death, and there was no one by me to support me ;
and, before I was allowed to go to his bedside, the
surgeon's steel and the blood-stained lint passed
through my hands.

Francesca Doni.

Yes, yes, true : your strength is great. Nothing
is too much for you. But think ; this is not the same
thing. It is not the same thing to go there, and to
find yourself face to face with a woman whom you do
not know, capable of anything, obstinate, impudent.

Silvia Settala.

I have no fear of her. What she does is base.
Because she thinks me weak and submissive, therefore
she is bold ; because I have so long remained silent,
and aloof, therefore she thinks she can once more get

the better of me. But she is wrong. Then all I cared for was lost, all resistance was useless. Now I have won it back, and I defend it.

FRANCESCA DONI.

My God! you are throwing yourself into a hand to hand contest. And if she resists?

SILVIA SETTALA.

How resists? I have my right. I can turn her out.

FRANCESCA DONI.

Silvia, Silvia, my sister, I entreat you; wait a few days longer, think it over a little before you do this. Do not be rash.

SILVIA SETTALA.

Ah, you speak well, you who are happy, you who are safe, you whose life is secure and with nothing to threaten your peace. Wait, think over! But do you know the crisis in which I find myself to-day? Do you know what I am fighting for? For my own self and for Beata, for existence, for the light of my eyes. Do you see? I cannot again go through a martyrdom in which all my nerves were torn to pieces; in which every torture was tried on me. I have given sorrow all I can give it; I have felt the hard iron on my

neck and on my wrists; at the day's end my sleep was
taken away by the horror of the day to come, in which
I should have to go on living, and, in order to live,
squeeze out my heart drop by drop when it seemed
empty of everything.　Ah, you speak well, you!
When you smile in your home your smile returns to
you in a hundred rays, as if you lived in a crystal.
For me, smiling was one sorrow the more; under it,
I clenched my teeth; but Beata never saw a tear in
my eyes.　That I might fulfil the promise of her
name, when there was not a fibre in me that was not
wrenched asunder, my hands were always held out to
her with flowers.　I could not begin over again.　I would
rather go away myself, and find a little quiet seashore
somewhere, and lie down there with Beata and let the
sea take us.

FRANCESCA DONI.

[*Throwing her arms around her sister's neck, and
kissing her.*] What are you saying? what are you
saying?　You ought to be afraid of nothing any longer.
Does he not love you?　Have you not seen all his love
come back?　That is what matters; all the rest is
nothing.

　　　　[SILVIA *closes her eyes for a few instants, and the
　　　　　illusion brightens her face.*

Yes, yes, I have seen his love come back. It
seems . . . How could I doubt that voice? When
I am not there, he calls me, he looks for me; he
needs me; it seems as if I am to lead his steps.

[*She shakes herself, withdraws from her sister's*
arms, and becomes anxious again.

But to-day. . . . Did you see him? did you look at him?
To-day he is not like he was yesterday. A sudden
change. . . . Did you look at him when he was at the
window, leaning out? Did you hear the sound of his
words? Did you see how his arm trembled when he
stretched it out? Ah, tell me if you too felt that
something had happened, that something had disturbed
him.

FRANCESCA DONI.

He is still convalescent. Think; a mere nothing is
enough to disturb him, the air, the weather . . .

SILVIA SETTALA.

No, no, it is not that. And did you not see?
Cosimo Dalbo too seemed to be making an effort to
hide some shadow. My eyes never deceive me.

FRANCESCA DONI.

No, it did not strike me. He was talking with me.

SILVIA SETTALA.

[*With increasing agitation.*] But Lucio went down
to see him out, and he has not yet come back.   Or
perhaps he went across to the other side.

> [*Goes to the window, and looks through the cur-
> tains.*

Ah, he is still there, at the gate, talking, talking.   He
seems beside himself.   [*Lifts her eyes to the clouds.*
The thunder is coming. [*Looks out again, very intently.*

FRANCESCA DONI.

Call him !

SILVIA SETTALA.

[*Turning, as if seized by a terrible thought.*]   I am
sure of it, I am sure of it.

FRANCESCA DONI.

What are you thinking of now ?

SILVIA SETTALA.

[*Pausing, and pronouncing the words distinctly, pale
but resolute.*] Lucio knows that she is waiting for
him.

FRANCESCA DONI.

He knows ?   How ?

SILVIA SETTALA.

There is no doubt, there is no doubt.

FRANCESCA DONI.

You imagine it.

SILVIA SETTALA.

I feel it; I am sure of it.

FRANCESCA DONI.

But how?

SILVIA SETTALA.

It was bound to come; she was bound to find out
the way one day or another. How? A letter,
perhaps. He has received a letter.

FRANCESCA DONI.

And you were not on the watch?

SILVIA SETTALA.

[*Disdainfully.*] Even that?

FRANCESCA DONI.

But perhaps you are mistaken.

SILVIA SETTALA.

I am not mistaken. After the old man's visit, she

wrote. Delay is no longer possible now, not a day,
not an hour. You see the danger. Though he may
have come back to me with all his soul, though he
may have broken with her entirely, though he may
have gone back to another life, another happiness, do
you not feel what might still be the fascination for him
of a woman who says, obstinate and certain : " I am
here, I wait " ? To know that she is there, that she
is waiting there every day, that nothing can dishearten
her. Do you see the danger ? If Lucio knew this morning that she is waiting for him, he must know to-night,
and from my lips, that she waits for him no longer.

> [*An indomitable energy strengthens and lifts
> her whole being.*

He shall know it to-night ; I promise him.

> [*She stretches out her hand towards the window,
> with the gesture of one taking an oath.*

Will you come with me ?

FRANCESCA DONI.

[*Anxious and entreating.*] Silvia, Silvia, think for
one moment ! Think what you are doing !

SILVIA SETTALA.

I do not ask your aid. I only ask you to come with
me as far as the door. For the rest, I alone suffice ;

it is necessary that I should be alone. Will you?
What time is it?

> [*Turns to look at the time; goes towards the table.*

FRANCESCA DONI.

[*Stopping her.*] I entreat of you! Listen to me,
Silvia! My heart tells me that no good can come of
what you are wanting to do. Listen to your sister!
I entreat of you.

SILVIA SETTALA.

[*With a gesture of impatience.*] Don't you know the
game I am playing? Let me be. I am going alone.
[*Bends over the table, and looks at the time.*] Four
o'clock. I have not a moment to lose. Is your
carriage there?

> [*The rain falls suddenly on the trees in the garden.*

FRANCESCA DONI.

See how it is pouring! Don't go out! Put it off
till to-morrow. Come, listen. [*Tries to draw her
towards her.*] Wait at least till it stops raining.

SILVIA SETTALA.

I have not a minute to lose. I must be there
before her; she must find me there as if in my own

house. Do you understand? Let me go. Quick, my hat, my cloak, my gloves. Giovanna!

> [*She goes into the next room calling to her maid.*
> FRANCESCA DONI, *terrified, goes towards the window, on which the rain is beating.*

FRANCESCA DONI.

My God! my God! [*Looks into the garden ; calls :* Lucio! Lucio!

> [*Turns towards the door through which her sister has gone out.*

SILVIA SETTALA.

[*Coming back, out of breath.*] I am ready. I left Beata there in tears. She wanted to go out with me. Stay, please ; go and comfort her. I will go alone. I shall take your carriage. *Au revoir.*

> [*Is about to kiss her sister.*

FRANCESCA DONI.

You are going, then? You have decided?

SILVIA SETTALA.

I am going.

FRANCESCA DONI.

I will go with you.

SILVIA SETTALA.

Let us go.

> [*Involuntarily she turns and looks around the room, as if to embrace everything that is in it in one look. The curtains tremble, the rain increases. She breathes in the damp fragrance that enters at the window. For one instant the strung bow of her will slackens.*

The odour of the earth . . .

> [*She shivers, as she suddenly catches sight of* LUCIO, *who appears on the threshold, feverishly, with bare head, his hair and his clothes wet with rain. They look at one another. An interval of weighty silence.*

LUCIO SETTALA.

[*In a hoarse voice.*] You are going out ?

SILVIA SETTALA.

Yes, I am going out.

LUCIO SETTALA.

How pale you are ! [SILVIA *puts her hand to her throat.*] Where are you going ?   It is a deluge.

> [*He touches his dripping hair.*

F

SILVIA SETTALA.

I have to go out. I shall not be long. Beata is in there, crying because she wants to come with me. Go and comfort her, tell her that perhaps I will bring her back something beautiful.

> [LUCIO *suddenly takes her hands and looks her fixedly in the eyes.*

SILVIA SETTALA.

[*Mistress of herself, with a clear and firm accent.*] What is it, Lucio ?

> [*He casts down his eyes. She withdraws her hands, shaking his as if in a farewell greeting. The temper of her will rings out in her vivid voice.*

Au revoir! Come, Francesca. It is time.

> [*She goes out rapidly, followed by her sister.* LUCIO SETTALA *remains with bowed head, staggering under a thought that transfixes him.*

END OF THE SECOND ACT.

THE THIRD ACT

A high and spacious room, lighted by a glass roof,
covered with dark awnings. In the wall at th
back there is a rectangular opening, somewhat
larger than a door, leading into the sculptor's studio.
On the architrave are some fragments of the frieze
of the Parthenon ; against the two sides are two
large winged figures, " clothed with the wind," the
Nike of Samothrace and the other Nike sculptured
by Pæonius for the Doric temple of Olympia
consecrated to Zeus; the opening is covered by a
red curtain.

In the left wall there is a door, hidden by a rich
and heavy portière ; in the left, a little door is
hidden by curtains. Wide divans, covered with
cloths and cushions, surround the room. The
figures are arranged carefully, as if to induce
meditation and reverie : a bunch of corn in a copper
vase stands before the Eleusinian bas-relief of

*Demeter ; a little bronze Pegasus on a pedestal of
"verde antico" stands before the Ludovisi Medusa.*
The *sentiment expressed by the aspect of the place
is very different from that which softens the aspect
of the room in the other house, over against the
mystic hill. Here the choice and analogy of every
form reveals an aspiration towards a carnal, vic-
torious, and creative life. The two divine mes-
sengers seem to stir and widen the close atmosphere
incessantly with the rush of their immense flight.*

SCENE I.

SILVIA SETTALA *stands in the middle of the room, having
laid down her hat, cloak, and gloves. She seems
trying to remember the things about her, almost to
renew her acquaintance with them, to re-establish a
communion with them, not to feel estranged from
them. She represses her anguish under her sister's
eyes.* FRANCESCA DONI *is seated, because her knees
tremble and her heart beats too loud.*

SILVIA SETTALA.

[*Looking about her.*] It is strange ; it seems larger.

FRANCESCA DONI.

What ?

SILVIA SETTALA.

The room.　It doesn't seem the same.

[*She looks about her, as if breathing an unfamiliar
air.　An interval of silence.*

FRANCESCA DONI.

[*Listening.*]　Did you shut the door ?

SILVIA SETTALA.

Yes, I shut it.

FRANCESCA DONI.

We shall hear her open it.

SILVIA SETTALA.

Are you afraid ?　It is not time yet.　In a minute
you must go.

FRANCESCA DONI.

Where ?

SILVIA SETTALA.

Will you wait for me in the carriage, in the
street ?

FRANCESCA DONI.

No, it is impossible.　I want to be here, to be near
you.　Could I not hide myself ?

SILVIA SETTALA.

Hide yourself, here? No. I must be alone.

FRANCESCA DONI.

Have pity on me ! I shall die of suspense.

SILVIA SETTALA.

Wait. There ought to be a secret door here.
  [*Guided by memory, she goes towards the wall
    where there is the hidden door ; looks, finds it,
    opens it. A wave of light falls over her.*
Do you see! It goes from here into the model's
room, then into a corridor. At the end of the corridor
there is a door, which leads to the Mugnone. Will
you go out that way ?

FRANCESCA DONI.

Yes, but let me stay in the room or the corridor
and wait. I will wait till you call.

SILVIA SETTALA.

You promise to wait till I call ?

FRANCESCA DONI.

Yes, I promise.

SILVIA SETTALA.

Do not fear. See, there is the sun on the window.

> [*Both look out through the half open door. The inner light shines on their faces. A luminous streak extends over the floor.*

FRANCESCA DONI.

It is not raining now. Look at all the primroses on the roadside.

SILVIA SETTALA.

Go and wait on the roadside, in the open air. Go.

FRANCESCA DONI.

There is an old sick horse, with his legs in the water. Do you see ? And the swallows skim across it. I think . . .

> [*She starts and turns suddenly, gazing at the motionless folds of the portière.*

SILVIA SETTALA.

What is it ?

FRANCESCA DONI.

I thought I heard . . .

> [*Both listen.*

SILVIA SETTALA.

No, you are mistaken. It is still early. And then

the door on the stairs makes a great noise when it
closes.   Did you not hear it when we came in ?   The
walls tremble.

FRANCESCA DONI.

[*Imploringly.*]   Silvia !

SILVIA SETTALA.

What is it now ?

FRANCESCA DONI.

Listen.   There is still time.   Come away, come
away at least for to-day !   Try, at least.   She will
know you have been here.   We will speak to the
caretaker again.   You ought to leave some sign here,
forget a glove, for instance.   She will understand,
she will not return.

SILVIA SETTALA.

A glove enough ?   Ah, how easy everything is for
your heart !

[*She looks round her again, with a secret despair.*
There is nothing left of me, here.

[*The sister remains by the half open door, her
figure partially lit up by the vivid reflection.
Silvia moves some paces into the room.   An
interval of silence.*

Everything seems larger, higher, darker.

FRANSESCA DONI.

It is the shadow that deceives you. There is not
much light. Draw back the awning over the sky-
light.

SILVIA SETTALA.

No, it is better like this.

[*She looks in every corner, as if seeking a trace.*
Tell me . . .

[*Her voice chokes with emotion.*

That night they came for you, and you hurried
here. You were here at the very beginning . . .

[*Hesitates.*

Where was he ? Do you remember exactly where ?

FRANCESCA DONI.

There, in the studio, under the statue. No, do not
go!

[SILVIA *turns towards the red curtain that hangs
between the two Victories. At her feet, like a
dividing line, stretches the thin zone of the
sun.*

SILVIA SETTALA.

[*In a low voice.*] The statue is there.

FRANCESCA DONI.

Do not go !

[S*ILVIA remains for some instants motionless
and silent before the closed curtain, from
which she is separated by the shining zone.*

Do not go!

[S*ILVIA steps across the sunlight, almost violently,
as if to overcome an obstacle; with a rapid
movement she raises the curtain, slips between
the folds, and disappears. The curtain falls
behind her, heavy and . thick. There are a
few instants of silence, in which nothing is
heard but the rapid breathing of the sister.
Suddenly, within the purple depths, appears
the white face of Silvia, which seems irradiated
with the light of the masterpiece. Her bare
hands, as they put aside the curtains, seem
to shine against the depths of colour. Her
eyes are intent, widened by wonder, dazzled,
not by a vision of death, but by an image of
perfect life. The water gathers tremulously
in her eyes. Two marvellous tears form little
by little, shine, and slowly run down her
cheeks. Before they reach her mouth she stops
them with her fingers, diffuses them over her
face, as if to bathe in lustral dew; for it is
not by the remembrance or the trace of human
bloodshed that she is moved, but by the sight*

of a thing of beauty, solitary and free. She
has received the supreme gift of beauty : a
truce to anguish, a pause to fear. The
sublime lightning-flash of joy has shone
through her wounded soul for an instant,
rendering it crystalline as tears. These tears
are but the soul's mute and ardent offering
before a masterpiece.

Silvia, Silvia, you are weeping.

SILVIA SETTALA.

[*In a subdued voice, with a gesture of silence.*] Hush !
   [*She moves away from the curtain, asking in a*
     subdued voice :

Have you seen ? have you seen ?

FRANCESCA DONI.

[*Misunderstanding, with a start.*] Who ? Her ? Is
she there ?

SILVIA SETTALA.

No, the statue.
   [*The sister nods her head, with a gesture expressing*
     rapt admiration. The sound of a heavy door
     closing is heard. Both start.

She is here. Go, go.

FRANCESCA DONI.

[*Holding out her arms towards her with a last agonised
.entreaty.*] Oh, my sister!

SILVIA SETTALA.

[*Recovering her former energy.*] Go! Do not fear.
  [*She pushes her sister out through the door, and
    closes it. The zone of sun disappears; the
    room returns to an even shadow.*

SCENE II.

.SILVIA SETTALA *is standing with her face turned
    towards the door, her eyes fixed, almost rigid in ex-
    pectation. Through the profound silence is heard
    distinctly the turning of the key in the lock.*
    SILVIA'S *attitude does not change. A hand lifts
    the portière.* GIOCONDA DIANTI *enters, closing the
    door behind her. At first she does not perceive the
    adversary, since she comes from the light into the
    shadow and a thick veil covers her whole face.
    When she perceives her, she stops, with a choked cry.
    Both remain for some instants facing one another
    without speaking.*

SILVIA SETTALA.

[*With a firm and clear accent, but without resentment or menace.*] I am Silvia Settala.

[*Her rival is silent, still veiled. A pause.*] And you?

GIOCONDA DIANTI.

[*In a low voice.*] Do you not know, Signora?

SILVIA SETTALA.

[*Still restraining herself.*] I know only that you have entered here, as into a place that belongs to you. You find me here, as in my own house. One of us two, therefore, usurps the right of the other; one of us two is the intruder. Which? [*A pause.* I perhaps?

GIOCONDA DIANTI.

[*Always hidden under the veil, and in a low voice, as if to lessen her audacity.*] Perhaps.

[SILVIA SETTALA *turns paler and staggers a little, as if she had received a blow.*

SILVIA SETTALA.

[*Resolutely, quivering with disdain.*] Well, there is a woman who has drawn a man into her net with the worst allurements; who has torn him away from the

peace of home, the nobility of art, the beauty of a
dream which he had nourished for years with the
flowers of his force ; who has dragged him into a turbid
and violent delirium, where he has lost all sense of goodness and justice ; who has inflicted on him the sharpest
torments that the cruelty of a torturer sick with
ennui could desire ; who has exhausted and withered
him up, keeping a perverse fever continually alight in
his veins ; who has rendered life intolerable to him ;
who has armed his hand and turned it against his
own life ; who in short, has known that he was lying
wounded to death on a far-off bed, for days and days,
while a ceaseless fight went on about him against death ;
and who has not had remorse, nor pity, nor shame, but
has gone back to the sinister place before the blood
was wiped off the floor, meditating another attack upon
her prey, awaiting him again at the journey's end,
calculating one by one the effects of her temerity
and of her tenacity, promising herself the pleasure
of another ruin. There is a woman who has done
this, who has said : " A strong and noble life
flourished freely in the world ; I have seized it, bent
it back, beaten it down, then shattered it at a blow. I
thought I had destroyed it for ever. And lo! it
flourishes again, is renewed, re-arises, can put forth
fresh flowers ! About it the wounds close, the pains

are calmed, hope springs up again, joy can smile!
Shall I endure this wrong? Shall I let myself be thus
deluded? No, I will begin again, I will hold on, I
will overcome all resistance, I will be implacable."
There is a woman who has promised this to herself,
who has gripped her will like an axe, who is prepared to deliver fresh blows smiling. Do you know
her? She has entered here with her face covered, she
has spoken in a dull voice, she has let fall a cold word,
calculating always on her own audacity and on the
other's submissiveness. Do you know her?

GIOCONDA DIANTI.

[*Without changing her manner.*] She whom I know
is different. Only because she is sad in your presence,
does she speak in a low voice. She respects the great
and sorrowful love that has given you life; she admires
the virtue that exalts you. While you were speaking,
she understood that it was only in order to comfort
an unutterable despair that your words had created a
figure so different from the real person. There is
nothing implacable in her; but she herself obeys a
power that may be implacable.

SILVIA SETTALA.

[*Bitter and haughty.*] I know that you are practised
in all tongues.

GIOCONDA DIANTI.

Of what avail is this harshness ? Your first words
had another sound ; and it seemed, when you asked
me a question, that you wanted simply to know the
truth.

SILVIA SETTALA.

And what then is your truth ?

GIOCONDA DIANTI.

The truth that matters, between us, is one only :
truth of love. You know it. But I fear to wound.

SILVIA SETTALA.

Do not fear to wound.

GIOCONDA DIANTI.

The woman against whom you made such accusa-
tions was ardently loved, and—suffer me to say it!—
with a glorious love. She did not abase but exalt a
strong life. And since the last voice that she heard,
a few hours before the terrible deed was accomplished,
the last was of love, she believes that she is still
loved. And this is the truth that matters.

SILVIA SETTALA.

[*Blindly.*] She is wrong, she is wrong. . . You are

wrong! He loves you no longer, he loves you no
longer; perhaps he has never loved you. His
was not love but a poisoning, but sharp slavery, mad-
ness, and thirst. When he suffered on his pillow,
remembrance passed through his eyes from time to
time like a flash of terror. Weeping at my feet, he
has blessed the blood that was poured out for his
ransom. He does not love you, he does not love
you!

GIOCONDA DIANTI.

Your love cries out like a drowning man.

SILVIA SETTALA.

He does not love you! You have been a gad-fly
to him, you have made him frantic, you have driven
him to his death.

GIOCONDA DIANTI.

Not I, not I, have driven him to his death, but
you yourself. Yes, he wished to die, that he might
cast off a fetter, but not that which bound him to me:
another, yours, that which was set upon him by your
virtue or your rule, and which made him suffer
intolerably.

SILVIA SETTALA.

Ah, there is nothing that you dare not travesty!

G

From him, from his own mouth, in an hour when his
whole soul had risen up into the light, from him I
heard it : " If violence is enough to break a yoke, let
it be blessed ! " From him I heard it, when all his
soul opened again to the truth.

GIOCONDA DIANTI.

But here, a few hours before he gave way to the
horrible thought, here (all these things are witnesses
to it) he said to me the most ardent and the sweetest
words of all his love ; here he once more called me
life of his life, here he told me once more his dream
of forgetfulness, of liberty, of art, of joy. And here
he told me of the insupportableness of his yoke, the
inevitable weight of goodness, more cruel than any
other, and the horror of daily suffering, the repugnance at returning to the house of silence and tears,
the repugnance at length become unconquerable.

SILVIA SETTALA.

No, no. You lie.

GIOCONDA DIANTI.

To escape that anguish, one evening when all
seemed to him sadder and more silent than ever,
he sought death.

SILVIA SETTALA.

You lie, you lie! I was far away.

GIOCONDA DIANTI.

And you accuse me of having inflicted an infamous torment upon him, of having been his torturer! Ah, your hands, above all, your hands of goodness and pardon, prepared for him every night a bed of thorn, on which he could not lie down. But, when he entered here where I awaited him as one awaits the creating God, he was transformed. Before his work he recovered strength, joy, faith. Yes, a continual fever burned in his blood, kept alight by me (and this is all my pride); but the fire of that fever has fashioned a masterpiece.

[*Points towards her statue, hidden by the curtain.*

SILVIA SETTALA.

It is not the first; it will not be the last.

GIOCONDA DIANTI.

Truly, it will not be the last; because another is ready to leap forth from its covering of clay, another has palpitated already under the life-giving thumb, another is half-alive, and waits from moment to moment for the miracle of art to draw it wholly forth to the light. Ah, you cannot understand this impatience of matter to which the gift of perfect life has been promised!

> [SILVIA SETTALA *turns towards the curtain, takes a few steps, slowly, as if involuntarily, as if in obedience to a mysterious attraction.*

It is there; the clay is there. That first breath that he infused into it, I have kept alive from day to day, as one waters the furrow where the seed lies deep. I have not let it perish. The impress is there, intact. The last touch, which his feverish hand set upon it at the last hour, is visible there, energetic and fresh as yesterday, so powerful that my hope in the midst of all the agony of sorrow is set there with a seal of life, and takes strength from it.

> [SILVIA SETTALA *pauses in front of the curtain, as before, and remains motionless and silent.*

Yes, it is true, you watched by the bedside of the dying man, intent upon a ceaseless strife to win him back from death; and for this be envied, and for this be praised to all eternity. You had strife, agitation, effort : you had to accomplish a thing which seemed superhuman, and which intoxicated you. I, shut out, far off, in solitude, could only gather and bind up, knitting my will together, my sorrow in a vow. My faith was equal to yours; truly, it was leagued with yours against death. The last creative spark of his genius, of the divine fire that is in him, I have not let it go out, I have kept it alive, with a religious and uninterrupted vigilance. Ah, who can say to what height the preserving force of such a vow may attain?

[*SILVIA SETTALA is about to turn violently, as if to reply, but restrains herself.*

know, I know: it is simple and easy enough, what I have done; I know : it is no heroic effort, it is the humble duty of a menial. But it is not the act that matters. What matters is the spirit in which the act is accomplished; the fervour of it is all that matters. Nothing is more sacred than the work that begins to live. If the spirit in which I have watched over it can reveal itself to your soul, go and see! That the work may go on living, my visible presence is needful. Realising this necessity, you will understand how in replying " Perhaps " to a question, I wished to respect a doubt which might be in you, but which was not in me, which is not in me. You cannot feel at home here as in your own house. This is not a house. Household affections have no place here; domestic virtues have no sanctuary here.

This is a place outside laws and beyond common
rights. Here a sculptor makes his statues. He is
alone here with the instruments of his art. Now I
am nothing but an instrument of his art. Nature
has sent me to him to bring him a message, and to
serve him. I obey ; I await him to serve him still.
If he entered now, he could take up the interrupted
work which had begun to live under his fingers. Go
and see !

>[SILVIA SETTALA *stands before the curtain, with-
>out advancing. An increasing shiver shakes
>her whole body, betraying her inner agitation;
>while the words of her rival become more and
>more sharp and stinging, definite, and at last
>hostile. Suddenly she turns, panting, im-
>petuous, resolved upon the last defence.*

SILVIA SETTALA.

No. It is useless. Your words are too clever.
You are practised in all tongues. You transform
into an act of love and faith what is only an act of
policy or of treachery. The work that was interrupted
should have perished. With the same hand that had
impressed the sign of life upon the clay, with the
same hand he grasped the weapon and turned it

against his heart. He did not doubt that he had set the deepest of gulfs between himself and his work. Death has passed there, and has severed every bond. What was interrupted should be lost. Now he is born again, he is a new man, he aspires towards other conquests. In his eyes there is a new light; his strength is impatient to create other forms. All that is behind him, all that is on the other side of the shadow, has no longer any power or value. What does it matter to him that an old piece of clay should fall into dust ? He has forgotten it. He will find fresher pieces, into which to infuse the breath of his new birth, and to model into the image of the idea that now inflames him. Away with the old clay ! How could you profess to think that you were necessary to his art ? Nothing is necessary to the man who creates. All converges in him. You say that Nature sent you to him to bear him a message. Well, he has received it, he has understood it, and he has responded to it with a sublime expression. What other could he derive from you ? What other could you give him ? It is not given to man to attain twice the same summit, to accomplish twice the same prodigy. You are left there, on the other side of the shadow, far off, alone, on the old earth. He goes towards the new earth now, where he shall receive

other messages. His strength seems virgin, and the
beauty of the world is infinite.

GIOCONDA DIANTI.

[*Taken aback by the unexpected rigour which repels
her, becoming more acrid, more haughty than ever, and
with an air of defiance.*] I am living and am here ; and
he has found in me more than one aspect, and the
words still intoxicate me that he said when he spoke
to me of his vision, different every morning when I
come before him.   Up to yesterday, certainly, he did
not know that I was waiting for him ; and his uncon-
sciousness has deceived you.   But to-day he knows.
Do you understand ? He knows that I am here, that
I await him.   This morning a letter told him, a letter
which came into his hands, which he has read.   And
I am certain—do you understand ?—I am certain
that he will come.   Perhaps he is on the way, perhaps
he is near the door.   Shall we wait for him ?

       [*An extraordinary change comes over the face of
          Silvia.   It seems as if something strange and
          horrible enters into her.   She is like one
          suddenly caught in the coils, writhing in
          the fascination of the serpent, blindly.   The
          ancient fatality of deceit suddenly assails
          the soul of the pure woman, conquers and*

*contaminates it. At the last words of the enemy
she breaks into an unexpected laugh, bitter,
atrocious, provocative, that renders her un-
recognisable. Gioconda Dianti seems overcome by it.*

SILVIA SETTALA.

Enough, enough. Too many words. The game
has lasted too long. Ah, your certainty, your pride!
But how could you believe that I should have come
here to contest the way with you, to forbid your
entrance, to face your audacity, if I had not had a
certainty far more sound than yours to warrant me?
I know your letter of yesterday, it was shown to me,
I know not if with more astonishment or disgust.

GIOCONDA DIANTI.

[*Overcome.*] No, it is not possible!

SILVIA SETTALA.

Yes, it is so. As for the answer, I bring it. Lucio
Settala has lost the memory of what has been, and
asks to be left in peace. He hopes that your pride
will prevent you from becoming importunate.

GIOCONDA DIANTI.

[*Beside herself.*] He sends you? he himself? It is his answer? his?

SILVIA SETTALA.

His, his. I would have spared you this harshness if you had not forced me. Will you go now?

GIOCONDA DIANTI.

[*Her voice hoarse with rage and shame.*] I am turned out?

> [*Fury suffocates her, and gives her a frantic rigour. The vindictive and devastating wild beast seems to awaken in her. Through her flexible and powerful body passes the same force which contracts the homicidal muscles of feline animals in ambush. The veil, which she has kept on her face like a dark mask, renders more formidable the attitude of one ready to do injury in any way and with any weapon.*

Turned out?

> [SILVIA SETTALA *stands convulsed and livid before the furious woman, and it is not the spectacle of that fury which terrifies her, bu*

something which she sees within herself, some-
thing horrible and irreparable : her lie.

Ah, you have brought him to this ! How ? how ?
Binding the soul like the wound with cotton-wool ?
doctoring him with your soft hands ? He is un-
made, finished, a useless rag. I understand ; now I
understand. Poor thing ! poor thing ! Ah, why is
he not dead, rather than the survivor of his soul ?
He is finished, then, a poor beggar whom you lead by
the hand in the empty streets. All is destroyed,
all is lost. He will never lift his head again, his eye
is darkened.

SILVIA SETTALA.

[*Interrupting her.*] Be silent, be silent ! He is living and strong ; never had he such light in himself.
God be praised !

GIOCONDA DIANTI.

[*Frantically.*] It is not true. I, I was his strength,
his youth, his light. Tell him ! Tell him ! He has
become old ; from to-day he is limp and soulless. I
carry away with me (tell him !) all that was most free,
ardent, and proud in him. The blood that he poured
out there, under my statue, was the last blood of his
youth. What you have re-infused into his heart is

without flame, is weak, is vile. Tell him! I carry
away with me to-day all that was his power and his
pride and his joy and his all. He is finished. Tell
him!

> [*Fury blinds and suffocates her. It is as if she
> is invaded by a turbid destructive will, as by
> a demon. All her being contracts in the
> necessity of accomplishing an immediate act
> of destruction. A sudden thought precipitates
> that instinct towards an aim.*

And that statue which is mine, which belongs to me,
which he has made out of the life that I have shed
from me drop by drop, that statue which is mine. . .

> [*She rushes like a wild beast towards the closed
> curtain, raises it and passes through.*

. . . well, I will shatter it, I will cast it down!

> [SILVIA SETTALA *utters a cry, and rushes forward
> to prevent the crime. Both disappear behind
> the curtain. The rapid breathing of a brief
> struggle is heard.*

SILVIA SETTALA.

[*Crying out.*] No, no, it is not true, it is not true!
I lied!

> [*The despairing words are covered by the sound of
> a mass that inclines and falls, the fracture of*

*the falling statue ; then follows another lacer-
ating cry from Silvia, torn by agony from
her very vitals.*

SCENE IV.

FRANCESCA DONI *appears, mad with terror, running
towards the cry, which she recognises ; while GIO-
CONDA DIANTI is seen between the curtains, still
veiled, in the attitude of one who has committed a
murder and seeks to escape.*

FRANCESCA DONI.

Assassin ! Assassin !

> [*She stoops to succour her sister, while the other
> rushes out.*

Silvia, Silvia, my sister, my sister ! What has she
done to you, what has she done to you ? Ah, the
hands, the hands. . . .

> [*Her voice expresses the horror of one who sees
> something frightful.*

SILVIA SETTALA.

Take me away ! Take me away !

FRANCESCA DONI.

My God, my God! They were underneath! My God! They are crushed! Water! water! There is none here. Wait.

SILVIA SETTALA.

Ah, what agony! I cannot bear it: I am dying. Take me away!

> [*She appears between the red curtains, her face inexpressibly contracted by agony, while her sister bends to support her two hands wrapped in a piece of wet cloth, taken from the clay, through which the blood oozes.*

What agony! I cannot bear it any longer.

> [*She is about to faint, when all at once* LUCIO SETTALA *rushes into the room like a madman. She trembles, fixing on him her great eyes full of tears, in which her despairing soul dies.*

You, you, you!

FRANCESCA DONI.

> [*Still supporting the two poor crushed hands that drench the cloth in which the incurable wreck is hidden.*

Support her, support her! She is falling.

> [LUCIO SETTALA *supports the poor bleeding creature,*

almost fainting, in his arms. But, before losing consciousness, she turns her glazing eyes towards the curtains as if to indicate the statue.

SILVIA SETTALA.

[*In a dying voice.*] It . . . is safe.

END OF THE THIRD ACT.

THE FOURTH ACT

*A ground floor room, white and simple, with two side
walls making an angle, almost entirely open to the
light, which comes through a sort of large window,
after the manner of a tepidarium. The blinds are
raised, and through the window-panes can be seen
oleanders, tamarinds, rushes, pines, golden sands
dotted with dead seaweed, the sea calm and dotted
with lateen sails, the peaceful mouth of the Arno,
beyond the river the wild thickets of Gombo, the
Cascine di San Rossore, the far off marble mountain
of Carrara.*

*A door, leading to the interior, is on the third side. By
the side of the door, on a bracket, is the Lady with
the bunch of flowers, the famous figure of Andrea
del Verrocchio, a new guest, come from the other
house, like a faithful companion, whose beautiful
hands are always flawless, as they make a graceful*

*gesture towards the heart. On the other side is an
old spinet, of the time of Elisa Baciocchi, Duchess
of Lucca, with its case of dull wood inlaid with
bright wood, borne by little gilded Cariatides in
the Empire style, with its four pedals united in the
form of a small harp.
It is an afternoon in September. The smile of
vanishing summer seems to lay an enchantment
over everything. In the deserted room the soul of
music sleeping in the forgotten instrument makes
itself felt, as if the hidden strings were touched by
the calm rhythm of the neighbouring sea.*

SCENE I.

SILVIA SETTALA *appears on the threshold, from the
inner room ; she pauses ; takes several steps
towards the window ; looks into the distance, looks
about her with infinitely sad eyes. In her way of
moving there is a sense of something wanting,
calling up a vague image of clipped wings, a
vague sentiment of strength humbled and shorn,
of nobility brought low, of broken harmony. She is
dressed in an ash-coloured gown, with a hem of*

H

*black, like a thread of mourning. Long sleeves
hide her arms without hands, which she sometimes lets drop by her side, and sometimes sets
together, drawn a little back, as if to hide them
in the folds, with a movement of shame and
sorrow.*

*From outside, between the thick oleanders, appears a
girlish figure,* LA SIRENETTA, *half fairy and
half beggar girl, peering in. She glides towards
the window with a furtive step, holding up in one
hand a fold of her apron filled with seaweed,
shells, and star-fish.*

SILVIA SETTALA.

[*Catching sight of her, and going towards her with a
smile.*]   Oh, la Sirenetta! Come, come.

LA SIRENETTA.

[*Coming forward to the window.*]   Do you remember
me?

> [*She remains outside so that her face is seen
> through the shimmer of the glass, which seems
> to continue about her the incessant, tremulous
> radiance of the sea. She is young, slender,
> graceful; her yellow hair is in disorder, her*

*face the colour of ruddy gold, her teeth
white as the bones of the cuttle-fish, her eyes
humid and sea-green, her neck long and thin,
with a necklace of shells about it; in her
whole person something inexpressibly fresh
and glancing, which makes one think of a
creature impregnated with sea-salt, dipped in
the moving waters, coming out of the hiding-
places of the rocks. Her petticoat of striped
white and blue, torn and discoloured, falls
only just below the knees, leaving her legs
bare; her bluish apron drips and smells of
the brine like a filter; her bare feet, in
contrast with the brown colour that the sun
has given her flesh, are singularly pallid, like
the roots of aquatic plants. And her voice is
limpid and childish; and some of the words
that she speaks seem to light up her ingenuous
face with a mysterious happiness.*

Do you remember me, pretty lady ?

SILVIA SETTALA.

I remember you ; I remember you.

LA SIRENETTA.

Do you remember me ? Who am I ?

SILVIA SETTALA.

Are you not la Sirenetta ?

LA SIRENETTA

Yes, you have remembered me.   When did you
come back ?

SILVIA SETTALA.

Not long ago.

LA SIRENETTA.

You will stay ?

SILVIA SETTALA.

A long time longer.

LA SIRENETTA.

Till the winter, perhaps.

SILVIA SETTALA.

Perhaps.

LA SIRENETTA.

And your little girl ?

SILVIA SETTALA

I expect her to-day.   She is coming.

LA SIRENETTA.

Beata !   Isn't she called Beata ?

SILVIA SETTALA.

Yes Beata.

LA SIRENETTA.

You called her that, Beata, not Beatrice. When she was here, she asked me every day for star-fish, stars of the sea. Did she tell you? She made me sing. Did she tell you?

SILVIA SETTALA.

Yes, she told me. She remembers you She likes you.

LA SIRENETTA.

She likes me! I know. She gave me some of her bread every day.

SILVIA SETTALA.

You shall have it every day, if you like. Bread and food, Sirenetta, morning and night, whenever you like. Remember.

LA SIRENETTA.

Morning and night I will bring you a star-fish. Will you have one? A pretty one, larger than a hand?

SILVIA SETTALA, *troubled, draws back her arms with an instinctive movement.*

Silvia Settala.

No, no, keep it for Beata.

La Sirenetta.

[*Surprised.*]   Won't you have it?

Silvia Settala.

Tell me instead what you do with your life, tell me
how you spend the day.   Is it true that you talk
with the sirens of the sea?   Tell me all about it,
Sirenetta.

La Sirenetta.

Seven sisters were we,
Our mirror the fountain-head,
All of us fair to see.
" Flower of the bulrush makes no bread,
Hedgerow mulberry makes no wine,
Blade of grass no linen fine,"
The mother to the sisters said ;
All of us fair to see,
And our mirror the fountain-head.
The first was fain to spin,
And wished for spindles of gold ;
The second to weave threads in,
And wished for shuttles of gold ;
The third to sew at her leisure,

And wished for needles of gold ;
The fourth to cook for her pleasure,
And wished for platters of gold ;
The fifth to sleep beyond measure,
And wished for dreams of gold ;
The sixth to sleep night away,
And wished for coverings of gold ;
The last to sing all day,
To sing for evermore,
And wished for nothing more.

[*She laughs with a quick glittering laugh that
seems to tinkle against her shining teeth.*

Do you like this story ?

SILVIA SETTALA.

[*Charmed by the grace of the simple creature.*] Is
that all ?   Why don't you go on ?

LA SIRENETTA.

If you sit here, I will put you to sleep as I put your
child to sleep on the sands.   Are you not sleepy now ?
Sleep is good, in September.

September bears to the plain
The windy breath of the mountain rain,
And puts the summer to sleep again.

Amen.

SILVIA SETTALA.

No.   Go on with your story, Sirenetta.

LA SIRENETTA.

The olive darkens for shedding,
Sorrow speeds the wedding,
Oil and tears wait for the treading.

SILVIA SETTALA.

Go on with your story, Sirenetta.

LA SIRENETTA.

Where had we got ?

SILVIA SETTALA.

"And wished for nothing more!"   [*A pause.*

LA SIRENETTA.

Ah, here it is :

     " Flower of the bulrush makes no bread,
     Hedgerow mulberry makes no wine,
     Blade of grass no linen fine,"
     The mother to the sisters said ;
     All of us fair to see,
     And our mirror the fountain-head.

And so the first one spun
Her own heart's woe for the morrow ;
And so the second wove,
And wove the cloth of sorrow ;
And so the third one sewed
A poisoned shirt to wear ;
And so the fourth one cooked
A dish of heart's despair ;
And so the fifth one slept
Under the coverings of death ;
And so the sixth one dreamt
In the arms of death.
The mother wept full sore,
And sighed away her breath ;
But the last, that only sang
To sing, to sing all day,
To sing for evermore,
Found her a happy fate.
[*She lowers her voice and makes it secret and
    remote.*
The sirens of the bay
Called her to be their mate.   [*A pause.*

SILVIA SETTALA

Then it is true that you talk with the sirens ?

LA SIRENETTA.

[*Putting her forefinger to her lips.*] Mustn't ask !

SILVIA SETTALA.

Is it true that no one knows where you sleep at night ?

LA SIRENETTA.

[*With the same gesture.*] Mustn't ask !

SILVIA SETTALA.

Shall I give you shelter, here in the house ?

LA SIRENETTA.

[*Looking intently in her face, as if she had not heard the question.*] Your eyes are sad. I did not know what troubled me when I looked at them. Now I see : you have a great sorrow in your eyes. Some one of yours is dead.

SILVIA SETTALA.

You alone can comfort me.

LA SIRENETTA.

Who of yours is dead ?

SILVIA SETTALA.

Mustn't ask !

La Sirenetta,

Now I see you: you are not the same. I was
thinking of a swallow, last September, who had lost
his longest feathers, and was nearly drowned in the
sea. What have they done to you? Something wicked
has been done to you.

Silvia Settala.

Mustn't ask !

> [*Instinctively she hides her arms without hands
> in the folds of her garment, with a sorrowful
> movement, which does not escape the notice of
> the bewitching creature; who suddenly, as if
> intentionally, drops the end of her apron, so
> that her little sea treasure falls and is scat-
> tered over the ground.*

La Sirenetta.

[*Stooping and choosing.*] Will you have a star-fish,
a pretty one, bigger than a hand? Look!

> [*She shows the mutilated woman a large sea-star
> with five rays.*

Take it ! I give it to you.

> [*The mutilated woman shakes her head in sign of
> refusal, pressing her lips together, as if to keep
> down the knot that tightens in her throat.*

Can't you ? Are your hands sick, tied up ?

[*The mutilated woman nods her head.* La
Sirenetta's *voice becomes tremulous with
pity.*

Did you fall into the fire ? Were you burnt ? Do
they still hurt ? Or are they getting better ?

Silvia Settala.

[*In a scarcely audible voice.*] I haven't any hands.

La Sirenetta.

[*Rising in affright.*] You haven't any ! They have
cut them off ? No hands ?

[*The mutilated woman nods her head, frightfully
pale. The other shivers with horror.*

No, no, no ! It isn't true.

[*She keeps her eyes fixed on the folds of the gar-
ment in which the mutilated woman hides her
arms.*

Tell me it isn't true.

Silvia Settala.

I haven't any hands.

La Sirenetta.

Why ? why ?

SILVIA SETTALA.

Mustn't ask!

LA SIRENETTA.

Ah, what a cruel thing!

SILVIA SETTALA.

I gave them away.

LA SIRENETTA

You gave them away ? To whom ?

SILVIA SETTALA.

To my love.

LA SIRENETTA.

Ah, what a cruel love! How beautiful they were,
how beautiful! Do you think I don't remember? I
have kissed them ; many many times. I have kissed
them with this mouth. They gave me bread, a pome-
granate, a cup of milk. They were as beautiful as
if the dawn had made them with a breath, as white
as the flower of the foam, more delicate than the
embroidery that the wind makes on the sand ; they
moved like the sun in the water, they talked better
than the tongue or the eyes, they said kind words,
what they gave turned to gold. I remember them!
I see them, I see them. One day they were playing

with the warm sand : the sand ran between the fingers
as through a sieve, and they were pleased at playing ;
and Beata looked at them and laughed ; and I looked
at them and had the same pleasure. One day they
peeled an orange ; and made it into many pieces, and
touched me with one of them, and it was as sweet as
a honeycomb. One day they wrapped a handkerchief
about the little one's foot, and she was crying because
a crab had nipped her, and the pain stopped all at
once, and the little one began to run along the shore.
One day they played with those lovely curls, and of
every curl they made a ring for every finger, and
then began over again, and then began over again ;
and Beata fell asleep with the dew on her lips.

SILVIA SETTALA.

[*In a choking voiee.*] Don't say any more! don't
say any more !

La SIRENETTA.

Ah, what a cruel love !

[*A pause.   She remains pensive.*]
And where are they ?   Far away, all alone, in the
earth, deep down.   Did they bury them ? Where ?   In
a pretty garden ?

[*A pause.   The mutilated woman shuts her eyes*

> *and leans her head against the window, in*
> *which the quiver of the sea is reflected.*

Did you see them taken away? How white they
were! They have wrapped them up in strong oint-
ment. And the rings? With all the rings? There
was one with a green stone, and one with three pearls,
and one of gold and iron twisted, and a smooth one, a
shining hoop, and only that one was on the third
finger.

> [*A pause. An indefinable expression appears on*
> *the face of the mutilated woman, as she lets*
> *her arms drop by her sides, while the rigidity*
> *of her whole body slackens.*

What are you thinking about? Dreaming of them?
If they should grow warm again. . . .

> [*The mutilated woman opens her eyes and*
> *starts, as if suddenly awakened. Her arms*
> *quiver.*

What is the matter?

SILVIA SETTALA.

It is strange. Sometimes it really seems to me as
if I have them again, I seem to feel the blood rise to
the tips of my fingers. When you spoke, I had them :
they were more beautiful, Sirenetta!

LA SIRENETTA.

More beautiful?

SILVIA SETTALA.

You will comfort me, Sirenetta. I cannot take
your star-fish, but I can see your eyes and hear your
voice. Keep near me, now I have found you again
I would like to have you for a sister.

LA SIRENETTA.

I would like you to have my hands, if they were
not so rough and dark.

SILVIA SETTALA.

Your hands are happy hands: they touch the
leaves, the flowers, the sand, the water, the stones,
children, animals, all innocent things. You are happy,
Sirenetta: your soul is born again every morning;
now it is little as a pearl, and now it is large as the
sea. You have nothing and everything; you know
nothing and everything.

LA SIRENETTA.

[*Turning suddenly and interrupting her.*] Did you
feel the gust? Look, look how many swallows on the

sea! There are more than a thousand : a living
cloud. Look how they shine! Now they are off;
they are going on a long journey, to a far away land ;
the shadow walks over the water with them ; some
feathers are falling : evening will come on ; they will
meet the ships on the high sea ; they will see the fires,
hear the songs of the sailors ; the sailors will see them
pass ; they will pass close to the sails ; one of them
will strike against the sails, and fall on the deck, tired.
One night, a cloud of tired swallows fell upon a ship
like a flock of starlings on the deck and quite covered
it. The sailors never touched them. They never
moved, for fear of frightening them ; they never
spoke, so that they might go to sleep. And as they
were all over the stock of the anchor and the bar of
the rudder, that night the ship went drifting under
the moon. But at dawn . . . Ah, who is calling to
you ?

> [*She interrupts her dream, hearing a strange
> voice among the oleanders; and prepares to
> fly.*

Good-bye, good-bye.

SILVIA SETTALA.

[*Anxiously.*] It is my sister. Do not run away, do
not go, Sirenetta. Stay here near. Beata is coming.

I

LA SIRENETTA.

Good-bye, good-bye. I will come back.

[*Runs towards the sea, vanishing into the sun-light.*

SCENE II.

FRANCESCA DONI *appears between the oleanders, followed by the old man,* LORENZO GADDI.

FRANCESCA DONI.

Do you see who I am bringing you ?

SILVIA SETTALA.

[*Anxiously.*] And Beata ? And Beata ?

FRANCESCA DONI.

She is coming presently. I left her with Faustina. I came beforehand, so that she should not come to you unexpectedly.

SILVIA SETTALA.

Dear Maestro, how pleased I am to see you !

[*The old man instinctively stretches out his*

*hands towards her. She bends slightly and
offers him her forehead, which he touches
with his lips.*

Lorenzo Gaddi.

[*Concealing his emotion.*] How happy I am to see
you again, dear Silvia, and to see you up and well
again! The sea helps you. The sea is always the
great comforter. At Forte dei Marmi, yonder, I
thought much of you.

Silvia Settala.

Is Forte dei Marmi far from here?

Lorenzo Gaddi.

[*Pointing to the distant shore.*] Yonder, under
Serravizza, on this side of Massa.

[*They look out of the window into the distance.*

Francesca Doni.

How well one can see the mountains of Carrara
to-day! You can count the peaks one by one. I
never remember a clearer day than this. Who was
with you, Silvia? La Sirenetta? I thought I saw

her running towards the sea.   And then here are her
traces : sea-weed, shells, star-fish.

> [*She points to the childish treasures scattered over
> the ground.*

SILVIA SETTALA.

Yes, she was with me just now.

LORENZO GADDI.

Who is la Sirenetta ?

FRANCESCA DONI.

A little wandering mad creature.

SILVIA SETTALA.

A seer, who has the gift of song ; a creature of
dream and truth, who seems a spirit of the sea.   You
should know her and love her as I do.   When you
know her and hear her speak, you find out many
deep things.   Truly she will seem to you perfect : she
always gives and never asks.

LORENZO GADDI.

She is like you in that.

SILVIA SETTALA.

Alas, no.   I should like to have been like her in
that ; but the light died away before the deceit of

life. What blindness! I asked so much, that to
obtain it, I stooped to tell a lie: I came out
mutilated, maimed, in punishment for my lie. I
had stretched out my hands too violently towards
a good thing that fate denied me. I do not
lament or weep. Since I must live, I will live.
Perhaps one day my soul will be healed. I felt some
hope arise in me, as I listened to the voice of that
simple and guileless creature who can teach eternal
things. She has promised to bring me a star-fish
every morning.

> [*She tries to smile. The sister stands near the
> window and seems to be looking intently at
> the distant mountains; but there is a shadow
> of sadness over her gentle face.* ·

Look, Maestro, at the lady with the bunch of flowers.
She has come with me. Now, if I look at her, there
is something mournful in her for me : all the same
I could not separate myself from her. Do you
remember, Maestro, that day in April, that garlanded
head ?

LORENZO GADDI.

I remember, I remember.

SILVIA SETTALA.

The new life!

LORENZO GADDI.

There was an omen in everything.

SILVIA SETTALA.

When I see the camels pass loaded with faggots, there, on the other side of the Arno, in the thickets of Gombo, I think of the arrival of Cosimo Dalbo, of the joy of that evening, of the scarabæus that I put in the midst of a bunch of roses that Beata had picked. [*Turns towards her sister.*] O Francesca, I speak, and all the while my heart troubles me so that I can resist no longer. Where is Beata?

FRANCESCA DONI.

[*Wrung with pain.*] You want to see her now? You are strong?

SILVIA SETTALA.

Yes, yes, I am strong, I am ready. Suspense is worse.

FRANCESCA DONI.

Then I will go and bring her to you.

SILVIA SETTALA.

[*Unable to contain her anxiety.*] Wait a minute.

Will you not stay with us here to-night, Maestro?
I should be glad.

LORENZO GADDI.

Well, yes, I will stay.

SILVIA SETTALA.

We can put you up. I will have your room got
ready. Wait, Francesca, a minute.

> [*She is convulsed with emotion, which she can no
> longer restrain. She goes towards the door
> like one who runs away to hide the tears that
> are about to break forth.*

FRANCESCA DONI.

Shall I come, Silvia?

SILVIA SETTALA.

[*With a choking voice.*] No, no.   [*Goes out.*

FRANCESCA DONI.

Ah, the curse, the curse ! Do you see her ? While
she was in bed, under the bedclothes, bound up,
bleeding, all the horror of the thing did not appear.
But now that she is on her feet again, now that she
moves, walks, sees her friends, returns to her old ways,

is about to use the gestures that she used to use!
Think of it!

LORENZO GADDI.

Yes, it is too frightful a fate. I remember what
you said to her so tenderly, as you looked at her, on
that day in April: "You seem as if you had wings!"
The beauty and lightness of her hands gave her the
aspect of a winged thing. There was in her a kind of
incessant quiver. Now it is as if she dragged herself along.

FRANCESCA DONI.

And it was a useless sacrifice, like all the others; it
has done nothing, changed nothing: that is where it
is so frightful a fate. If Lucio had stayed with her,
I believe she would have been happy to have been
able to give that last proof, to have been able to
sacrifice for him her living hands. But she knows
now all the truth, in all its nakedness. Ah, what an
infamous thing! Would you have believed that
Lucio was capable of it? Tell me.

LORENZO GADDI.

He too has his fate, and he obeys it. As he was
not master of his death, so he is not master of his life.
I saw him yesterday. He had written me at Forte

dei Marmi to ask me to go to the quarry and send him
a block   I saw him yesterday in his studio.   His
face is so thin that it seems burnt up in the fire of
his eyes.   When he speaks, he becomes strangely
excited.   It troubled me.   He works, works, works,
with a terrible fury : perhaps he is seeking to rid
himself of a thought that gnaws him.

FRANCESCA DONI.

The statue is still there ?

LORENZO GADDI.

It is still there, without arms.   He has left it so :
he would not restore it.   So, on the pedestal, it looks
really like an ancient marble, dug up in one of the
Cyclades.   There is in it something sacred and tragic,
after the divine immolation.

FRANCESCA DONI.

[*In a low voice.*]   And that woman, the Gioconda,
was there ?

LORENZO GADDI.

She was there, silent.   When one looks at her,
and thinks that she is the cause of so much evil,
truly one cannot curse her in his heart ; no, one

cannot, when one looks at her, I have never seen
so great a mystery in mortal flesh.

> [*A pause. The old man and the sister remain
> in thought, for some instants, with bowed
> heads.*

Francesca Doni.

[*Sighing because of the anguish that oppresses her.*]
My God, my God! And now it is time to bring
Beata to her mother, and they will see one another
again, after all that has happened ; and the little one
will learn the truth, will know the horrible thing.
How is one to hide it, from her, remembering all her
caresses, and mad for them ! You saw her, you
heard her, of old. . . .

> [Silvia Settala *reappears on the threshold. Her
> eyes are burning and all her body is con-
> tracted by a spasmodic force.*

Silvia Settala.

I am here, Francesca ; I am ready. The room is
ready, Maestro, if you would like to go to it.

Lorenzo Gaddi.

[*Going towards her, and in a voice trembling with
emotion.*] Courage ! It is the last ordeal.

[*He goes out by the door. The mutilated woman
  goes towards her sister, breathlessly.*

SILVIA SETTALA.

Now go, go ! Bring her.   I will wait here.
  [*The sister puts her arms round her neck and
   kisses her in silence.   Then she goes out
   towards the sea, and disappears rapidly
   among the oleanders.*

SCENE III.

SILVIA SETTALA, *breathlessly, looks through the midst
  of the boughs lighted by the oblique rays of the
  sun.   The hour is exquisitely peaceful.   The light
  is more limpid than the windows of the white
  room ; the sea is tranquil as the flower of the flax,
  so motionless that the long reflections of the mir-
  rored sails seem to touch the bottom ; the stream
  seems to create that immense repose, pouring out
  the perennial wave of its peace ; the health-giving
  woods, penetrated with fluid gold, rejoice marvel-
  lously, almost as if they lost their roots that they
  might swim in the delight of their odour ; the
  marble Alps in the distance trace a line of beauty*

*on the sky, in which they seem to reveal the dream
arising out of their imprisoned populace of sleeping statues.*

LA SIRENETTA *re-appears in the silence, through
which her pure voice is heard.*

LA SIRENETTA.

Are you alone ?

SILVIA SETTALA.

[*Agitated.*]   Yes. I am waiting.

LA SIRENETTA.

[*Coming close to her.*]   Have you been crying ?

SILVIA SETTALA.

Yes, a little.

LA SIRENETTA.

[*With infinite pity.*]   You seem as if you had been
crying for a year. Your eyes are burning. Your
heart hurts you too much.

SILVIA SETTALA.

Don't speak. I cannot crush my heart.

> [*She presses herself against the trunk of the
> nearest oleander, convulsed, no longer able to
> endure the agony of waiting.*

She is coming now. she is coming now.

> [*She moves away from the tree and re-enters the*

room, as if seized with terror, like one seeking·
refuge.

. THE VOICE OF BEATA.

[*From among the oleanders.*] Mamma ! Mamma !
[*The mother starts, and turns, frightfully pallid.*·
Mamma !

> [*The child rushes towards her mother with a cry*
> *of joy, her face lit up, heated, her hair in dis-*
> *order, panting after a long run, carrying an*
> *untidy bunch of flowers.   As she runs in, the*·
> *bunch falls.   The mutilated woman stoops*
> *towards the little arms that clasp her neck, and*
> *offers her death-like face to the furious kisses.*

SILVIA SETTALA.

Beata ! Beata !

BEATA.

[*Panting.*] Ah, how I have run, how I have run !·
I ran away from them, all alone.   I ran, I ran.   They
didn't want to let me come.   Ah, but I ran away from
them, with my bunch of flowers.

> [*Covers her mother's face with fresh kisses.*

SILVIA SETTALA.

You are all damp with sweat, you are hot, burning. . . My God !

[*In her rush of tenderness she instinctively makes a movement as if to wipe the child's face; but stops and hides her arms in the folds of her garments; and a shiver of visible horror runs through her.*

BEATA.

Why don't you take me up? Why don't you put your arms round me? Take me up, take me up, mamma!

[*She rises on tiptoe, to be caught into her mother's embrace. The mother takes a step backwards, blindly.*

SILVIA SETTALA.

Beata!

BEATA.

[*Following her.*] Don't you want me? don't you want me?

SILVIA SETTALA.

Beata!

[*She tries to feign a smile with her ashen lips, distorted by unspeakable sorrow.*

BEATA.

Is it for fun? What are you hiding? O, give, give me what you are hiding!

SILVIA SETTALA.

Beata! Beata!

BEATA.

I have brought you flowers, such a lot of flowers.
Do you see? do you see?

> [*As she turns to pick up the fallen bunch, she
> perceives her little wild friend, and remembers
> her.*

Oh, Sirenetta! Are you there?

> [LA SIRENETTA *is there, before the window, stand-
> ing, a silent witness, with her eyes fixed on the
> sorrowful mother. As the repeated breath of
> the wind passes between the fronds of an
> arbutus and makes it tremble, so the sorrow of
> the mother seems to invest and penetrate that
> slender body which the oblique rays of the
> sun ring with bands of gold.*

Do you see what a lot? All for you!

> [*The child picks up the bunch.*

Take it!

> [*She runs towards her mother again, who steps
> back.*

SILVIA SETTALA.

Beata! Beata!

BEATA.

[*Astonished.*] Don't you want them? Take them!
Take them!

SILVIA SETTALA.

Beata !

[*She falls on her knees, overcome with sorrow, as if stricken by an unendurable blow, falls on her knees before her frightened child : and a flood of tears, that bursts from her eyes like blood from a wound, bathes her face.*

BEATA.

You are crying ?   You are crying ?

[*Frightened, she throws herself upon her mother's breast, with all her flowers.* LA SIRENETTA, *who has also fallen on her knees, lays her forehead and the palms of her hands upon the ground.*

THE END.

Printed by BALLANTYNE, HANSON & Co.
London & Edinburgh